The view from Shenandoah looking west
across Pendleton County from near Reddish
Knob at the headwaters of the historic Potomac River.

The Potomac Naturalist

The Natural History

of

the Headwaters of the Historic Potomac

J. LAWRENCE SMITH

Photographs and drawings by the author

McCLAIN PRINTING COMPANY
PARSONS, WEST VIRGINIA 26287

1 9 6 8

For the People of the Potomac
and with special appreciation to
Maurice G. Brooks and Earl L. Core of West Virginia University
without whose instruction and inspiration
this book could have never been written

CONTENTS

INTRODUCTION

FROM THE VANTAGE POINT

Come with me to the crest of North Fork Mountain above the Smoke Hole in Pendleton County, West Virginia. We will climb the fire tower atop the mountain and make this our vantage point from which we can look across much of the three county area of Pendleton, Grant and Hardy as the mountains and valleys are unfolded before us towards the four points of the compass.

As we stand on the tower and look in various directions, we can see many of the prominent features in this region of the upper Potomac and with binoculars it is possible to bring many of these outstanding features into sharper focus for a closer view as we look at them across the distance of several air line miles. From our vantage point on the fire tower we can gain a vast and sweeping picture of the landscape, the mountains and valleys, and many prominent natural features in the upper Potomac region. It is possible to encompass so much from this point on top of the mountain as we focus our view of the mountainous landscape that will be the subject of the following pages.

Looking towards the south along the western side of North Fork Mountain, we can see Germany Valley. The name of the valley comes from the Pennsylvania Dutch settlers who were of German descent and moved into the valley, cleared the forests and began farming the rich soil. The River Knobs can be seen that rise abruptly along the western edge of the valley and separate the valley from the North Fork River and its course northward into Grant County. Towering above the course of the North Fork stands Seneca Rocks, but we cannot see this widely known natural feature in Pendleton County from our vantage point due to the mass of the mountain obstructing our view.

Shifting our view in a more westerly direction, we can see the massive ridge of Spruce Mountain. On this mountain is located the highest piece of solid ground in the state of West Virginia at Spruce Knob.

Towards the west we look into the great cleft in the mountain ridge that has been cut by Seneca Creek as it rushes from the mountain heights and flows into the North Fork River at Mouth of Seneca. Green Knob lifts its head above the other knobs in the west. U.S. route 33 can be seen winding its way up from the valley of the North Fork as it climbs the face of Allegheny Mountain before it drops down the mountain's back into Randolph County.

In the northwest we can see the long and flat-topped ridge of Allegheny Front Mountain with its patches of spruce. The land along the top of this mountain has been called the Roaring Plains since the wind often howls across the mountain's flattened top and the spruce trees bear the scars with their limbs blown to one side. With the use of binoculars, we can see the fire tower at Bell Knob as it perches near the edge of the mountain's steep flank.

As we look northward along the crest of North Fork Mountain, we see North Fork Gap where the North Fork River has cut a great gash in the spine of the mountain. Beyond the gap lies the high sandstone cliffs with their talus slopes where New Creek Mountain has its southern terminus. This mountain is a continuation of the same ridge as North Fork Mountain, but it has been given another name at this point because the river has forever broken the back of the mountain by cutting its course eastward through the gap.

Looking along the top of the mountain in a northerly direction, we see the high cliffs of Tuscarora sandstone that outcrop between our vantage point and North Fork Gap. This is the same hard sandstone that has been uplifted to form Seneca Rocks at Mouth of Seneca. In the distance just to the east of the mountain ridge, can be seen houses and barns in the neighborhood of Cabins west of Petersburg.

Moorefield, a town that has known a rich history and the wages of war with the ebb and flow of the armies of the North and South during the Civil War, is visible in the northeast. The ridge of South Branch Mountain rises beyond Moorefield and here at a high point on the mountain, the red pine grows and reaches one of the southernmost known places of growth for this northern pine. Not far from Moorefield, the outstanding feature of Baker Rock can be seen along with the other imposing palisades of Oriskany sandstone that are thrust upward from the mountain's flank. Eastward from Baker Rock lies the crest of Elkhorn Mountain.

As we look towards the east, it is possible to see the small community of Kline, to look through the Greenawalt Gap and beyond to South Fork Mountain. Beyond South Fork Mountain is the impressive ridge of Shenandoah Mountain, the mountain that has uplifted its high and lofty back to separate West Virginia from Virginia. Doubtless, the lofty ridge of Shenandoah Mountain which has often posed a barrier to transportation and communication was a prominent factor in Pendleton County and its people becoming a part of the state of West Virginia over one hundred years ago.

Casting our sights to the south, southeast along Shenandoah Mountain, we look towards Reddish Knob. Looking northward along the crest of the mountain, the fire tower above Brandywine can be seen and also the one at Cow Knob. Where the back of the mountain slumps, it is possible to see a ridge beyond which is probably North Mountain that separates Hardy County from Shenandoah County, Virginia. The clarity of the air and the great visibility from the vantage point are impressed upon us by the fact that we are looking at North Mountain at a crow flight distance of twenty-five miles.

As we stand on the fire tower and look across the landscape at the headwaters of the Potomac, let us take a brief journey through time and space to see the various changes that the passage of the seasons brings to the mountains and valleys.

During the months of winter, the land will be locked in cold and the spruce woods around Spruce Knob and along the Roaring Plains can be a most forbidding place for the winter adventurer. While much of the land will be held dormant in the firm grasp of winter, life will go on as usual for many animals and birds.

From our vantage point on a winter day when the land is snug beneath a blanket of snow and the trees on the mountain slopes in the distance stand out like strokes made with a charcoal stick, over the ridge we may hear the croaking of a raven on the chill, frosty air. Listening for awhile, we may hear other birds moving about in the naked trees seeking food to sustain the spark of life as they wait for the coming of a new season. We may hear a chickadee or nuthatch and even the hollow laugh of a pileated woodpecker as it calls and hammers somewhere down the slope. A flock of birds flying over the trees may prove to be evening grosbeaks, those big northern finches dressed in yellow and black that make their way south from time to time to spend the winter.

As the icy days of winter pass away and the heart of the earth is warmed by the lengthening days, spring will burst forth across the face of the land. The first wild flowers--arbutus, bloodroot, hepatica, fawn lily and spring beauty--burst through the litter on the forest floor and the dogwood will unfold its white flowers throughout the woods. The azaleas will soon add their lovely hues of rosy red and orange to the forests that are now deeply flushed with the green of new leaves. The trees will often seem alive with the abundance of birdlife as such birds as the warblers with their varied colors flash through the woods on their way north.

When spring becomes summer, there is a great variety of things to be found across the land. When one travels to Spruce Mountain or along the Allegheny Front, he will find a number of birds--golden-crowned kinglet, winter wren, Swainson's thrush, magnolia warbler and purple finch to mention a few--nesting in these localities which are characteristic species of the spruce forests of Canada. At the lower elevations, on the other hand, can be found birds that are characteristically birds of the South such as the loggerhead shrike and the black vulture.

At a number of places in the upper Potomac area, shales from the Devonian period of geological history can be found. On these shales and on similar soil at a few other places in the Alleghenies, grow a number of rare and interesting plants that can be found nowhere else in the world. On the shaly ground during June and July, the prickly pear cactus puts forth its bright yellow blossoms and brings a bit of the western deserts to these eastern mountains.

In the depths of the Smoke Hole, can be found a number of rare plants with one being the crested coralroot, an orchid that reaches the northern limits of its range in the Smoke Hole. Up from the Smoke Hole on the Tuscarora sandstone along the crest of North Fork Mountain and on this sandstone along other mountain ridges in the region, one can find the silvery whitlow-wort growing and here is a plant that grows nowhere else.

As the seasons again turn, nature paints its most beautiful picture across the face of the land with the rich and varied colors of fall. The trees seem aflame with crimson, scarlet, orange, gold and many other autumn hues that man with his synthetic dyes and colors has never been able to equal. From our vantage point, we would soon see riding the air currents and circling over the mountain ridge the hawks as they are flying southward from northern nesting grounds. As one watches the migration of the hawks on a day that is conducive to a good flight on the part of these birds of prey, one can see several hundred hawks of several species. If one is diligent in his observations, he may see such a magnificent and spectacular bird as the golden eagle.

Our trip through the seasons has come to an end as we have imagined some of the many varieties of plant and animal life and aspects of the geology that can be found at the headwaters of the Potomac. Many experiences in life are all too temporal, merely fleeting moments in the space of time and then they are gone. We cling to them with our memory, but even our memory fades, the image becomes less distinct and they are lost in the recesses of our mind. All things must pass away, but in the natural world there is the circle of the seasons to make the temporal border on the eternal.

The mountains are withering and moving towards the sea, but this withering is imperceptible and they will look the same long after

I am gone. The song of the veery that I long to hear may not be the same bird I heard last year, but the ethereal voice is the same. The events in a human life slip from our grasp, but the person who loves the land finds new sights and sounds to fill the gaps left by the old and to add color and meaning to a fading image of a similar thing.

All facets of the natural world are woven together by the bonds of many forces and in the terminology of the scientist this is properly known as ecology. This term means that all living things are dependent upon one another and are joined in their dependence by strands which might be compared to the silken threads of a web. When one strand of forces or factors is broken, the web is weakened and the whole may begin to unravel. I have attempted to follow the course of some of the threads in the web for a close look at the original wilderness scene, the geological history, the plant and animal life of the upper Potomac highlands.

It must be remembered that all aspects of the natural history of the region are dependent upon one another with the examples to illustrate this point being numerous. The present forest conditions are largely a result of the coming of the white man to the area. Many of the plants would not be found here if limestone had not been formed ages ago, nor would many of the birds nest here had the mountains not been uplifted. Through the vast interplay of forces throughout the ages, the present natural scene of the region has been brought into being. These are only a very few examples of the interdependence of the natural aspects of the region and many others will become apparent in the following pages.

It seems fitting at this point to make some comments about the preservation of the natural features in the upper Potomac region. The following pages are, to a great extent, a report on the state of natural things as I found them during the latter years of the seventh decade of the 20th Century. No one can say precisely what the years in the future hold for the region, but one can say that to a great extent the future of the natural variety and beauty of the upper Potomac lies with the people of the area.

While this region has not known the growing pains that have been experienced within recent years by many parts of our country, the time will eventually come when this region will be engulfed by expanding cities and the rapidly increasing population along the east coast as it moves westward from Washington, D. C. and the surrounding areas. Even though that day may be many decades away, there is a need for foresight and planning on the part of the people of the upper Potomac in order to preserve and maintain as found today the natural aspects of the region.

There is current in our nation a rather distorted view that pro-

gress can be measured in the glow of neon signs that blaze along a
highway and beckon one to come and eat, sleep, drink or make merry.
There would also be those people who would insist that progress can be
measured in the suburbs that sprawl across the countryside from many
cities or by the many thousands of automobiles that crowd the freeways
during the rush hour. This is a view of progress that has been brought
about by the materialism of our age.

Can it not be that with a reshuffling of our values and a refocus-
ing of our point of view that progress can be measured in the mainte-
nance of rich soil and healthy forests? The upper Potomac area cannot
measure progress in gaudy neon signs, sprawling suburbs and rush hour
traffic jams and these are among its greatest assets. The region can
measure its own type of progress in prosperous farms, vast forests,
clear air and clean water and unscarred mountains that beckon one to
come scale their heights and find solitude. Some of these resources
such as clean air and water have nearly ceased to exist within many of
the so-called progressive areas of our nation.

Whether the people of the region realize it or not, their home-
land is becoming ever-increasingly a haven for those people who seek
to escape for a brief period of time the hum and hustle of the cities
along the east coast and particularly the areas of Baltimore and Washington. Anyone who travels to the camping areas in the Smoke Hole or
at other places in the three county area, can count a number of automo-
bile license plates from Maryland, Virginia, Pennsylvania and a number
of other nearby states.

What do they come to do? They come to camp, to fish, to hunt,
to explore the many limestone caves, to study the plant and animal life
and they come especially to leave behind for several days or a few
weeks the bustling and busy cities where they live and make their living.
While many of the campers and tourists who come to the region may
add no great amount of money to the local economy since they often
bring the food and facilities they need, they come to enjoy and make use
of the natural aspects of the region whether it be catching a golden
trout, exploring Hellhole Cave, hunting deer or turkeys, searching out
the crested coralroot or simply camping for a few days in the peaceful-
ness of the Smoke Hole canyon.

Therefore it becomes necessary that if these people are to be
attracted to the area in the future, the natural aspects in their many
forms and varieties must be preserved intact. The region has received
much attention recently by the federal government as evidenced by the
visit of Secretary of the Interior Udall to the Spruce Knob area. While
some of the federal plans for the development of the Spruce Knob-
Seneca Rocks recreational area have been slowed by the recent war
effort in Southeast Asia, time is now the main factor involved in the

determination of when federal control and regulation of many key scenic and wild areas will be a reality. When the federal plans are realized, there will still be the need for a concern on the part of the local people in order for those valuable and irreplaceable natural things to be preserved for the many years to come in the future. Legislation and regulations will be of little value without the care and cooperation of all the people regardless of whether they be local people or visitors.

Pendleton County is indeed fortunate in having a tract of virgin forest that has been given protection by the Nature Conservancy. While many people might cast an appraising eye upon the vast amount of lumber found of this tract of land, there are many people from outside the county and state who will come to look and wonder at these trees that cast their massive trunks towards the sky. While the people of Pendleton County may take the forest resource for granted, at many places not far from the region one seldom sees a prosperous and thriving forest. The greatest value that the tract of virgin timber can have in the future is to grow and thrive and to offer to people a glimpse of the forests that were once spread like a great blanket of green across wilderness America. This is only one example of the variety of things that are to be found in the upper Potomac region, but natural objects that do not exist or ceased to exist years ago in other parts of our nation.

My bonds with the region are by adoption rather than by native birth. From the first day I came into the upper Potomac highlands bringing with me an almost insatiable interest in natural history, the avenues of exploration and discovery were open almost everywhere. The richness of things natural and the magnificent scenery hold me in the grasp of this land. These pages are written as a portrait of the impressions that the land has left with me during my search for its natural secrets along with the facts about its natural history. It is intended that these pages serve as an introduction to the natural history of a region of great natural diversity, an area rich in lore and legend and a mountainous land with unmatched vistas.

As we stand at our vantage point, it is now time to be on with the story of the land and wildlife at the headwaters of the historic Potomac River. The land will reveal its secrets to him who searches with expectation and attunes his eyes and ears to the pulse of the earth and the circle of the seasons. Looking towards the east where the everlasting sun has risen for eons, we look in the direction of the beginning of our story during historical times. This is where it was to begin for good and ill, from that day forth and for evermore, as the first white man cast his sights westward and began the march to see what promises or even paradise lay beyond the next mountain and up the next valley.

CHAPTER ONE

THE VIEW FROM SHENANDOAH

The day the first white man cast his eyes upon the upper reaches of the South Branch Valley may always remain lost to the pages of history. In those days the river was called Wappatomika by the Indians which meant "river of wild geese," but that first white man knew nothing of this. As he stood atop the mountain that was later to be called Shenandoah, the great undulations of the earth in mountains and valleys stretched across many miles until lost in the blue and haze of the far horizon. Turning away from the panorama spread before him, this trail blazer, adventurer, hunter looked again to the east and returned to tell of a land stretching as far as a man's imagination. Others followed until a name and a date were remembered for recording in history.

In a time lost in the dim reaches of human endeavor, other men of a different skin color came to this land from another direction. The arrow points, artifacts and burial sites found at various places up and down the valley leave no doubt that the land knew the tread of the Indian through many centuries. To the west of the valley, the famed Seneca Trail was the avenue of the Indians coming from and going to the north. Many legends are told about the Indians and the towering cliffs of Seneca Rocks. Tradition has it they smoked deer meat in a cave not far from present Upper Tract and gave the area the name Smoke Hole. Although fact is often hard to separate from fiction, that the Indians were here is an indisputable fact and that they were reluctant to let the land slip from their grasp was a fact errupting into one of the bloodiest chapters of our history.

The "Indian old fields" of early explorers and journalists near present Moorefield in Hardy County were an area of clearings in the otherwise unbroken forests which had been made by the red men long before the white man came. Many stories and traditions have been attached to the "old fields" that have come down to the present day. Accounts recorded in history tell of many Indian graves in the area

along with artifacts that were found. One such article was a pipe of fine
workmanship having a snake represented as coiled around the bowl.
Mention is also made of an enormous human jawbone in one of the
graves. Whether this was authentic or just the imagination of men in a
time when many believed in vanished races of giants will never be
known.

Mention has also been made of six burial mounds found in Pendleton County. One opened near Brandywine held seven skeletons ar-
ranged like the spokes of a wheel with the heads outward. Signs of vil-
lages and rings of earth that may have formed the bases for palisades
were in evidence until recently in the county. Much work remains to be
done by a trained archeologist in order to piece together from what
fragments that remain a picture of the first inhabitants of the county.
Much evidence of great value has been lost forever, but the experienced
eye of an archeologist could detect signs that would help fill the gaps in
our knowledge about the men who roamed our state long before the
coming of the white man.

From what work has been done in the region by archeologists,
the evidence would seem to indicate the mounds were built by a Hopewellian culture dating from 500 to 1000 A. D. This culture was somewhat distant from the main center of Hopewellian activity in the Ohio
Valley, but the evidence seems to show a relationship nevertheless.
The Hopewellian mound builders constructed earthworks and mounds
containing several burials with grave offerings such as elaborate artifacts of copper and mica. The culture gets its name from the site in
Ohio where it was first studied and described. These mound builders
preceded by centuries the Indians of the historical period.

Tradition holds that a band of Shawnees under the leadership of
Killbuck lived along the South Branch until 1754. Killbuck was a chief
of ability and a man who never forgot a person who had dealt him a
wrong. The early contacts with the whites seem to have been friendly,
but in the spring of 1754, the band moved towards the Ohio after being
visited by Indians from that region who urged them to join them and
escape the pressures of the white man. Even though they had left the
South Branch, many of them were to see the land again in the years
to come when they returned to seek revenge upon the settlers during
the conflict that would be known in history as the French and Indian
War.

When war began to flare with France in America, Virginia
looked to its vulnerable frontier with the result that a string of forts
was ordered built for defense. George Washington was called to take
command and made his headquarters at Winchester. Many of the forts
were poorly manned and ill-equipped to face an attack from Indians,
but those who watched and waited were courageous men indeed.

This was a time when individual acts of courage were performed that began to grow into legends. One morning before day-
break, seven Indians surrounded the cabin of Samuel Bingamon near
present Petersburg. Bingamon, his wife, mother, father and a hired
man were inside the cabin when the Indians fired a shot into the house
that slightly wounded Bingamon's wife before they burst through the
door. As they entered, Bingamon began swinging his rifle which broke
at the breech with the first blows. Five Indians soon lay dead after being beaten to death by Bingamon while the other two started to flee.
Bingamon picked up a rifle dropped by the party, shot one down and
finished him with a tomahawk. The other escaped and no doubt told
stories of the white devil who nearly finished him off along with the
others. Samuel Bingamon became a legend during his own lifetime,
but many others were not so fortunate.

No one will ever know exactly what happened at Fort Upper
Tract on the morning of April 27, 1758. All that is now known for certain is that Captain James Dunlap and twenty-one other defenders were
massacred and the fort burned by several Indians and possibly a few
French soldiers. The garrison at Fort Seybert across the mountain
fared better when attacked the following day. Although the fort was
surrendered and the defenders taken prisoners, many who withstood
the ordeals ahead lived to tell of the attack in later years.

The war came to an end and with its end much of the grave danger of frontier settlement had passed. The valley was settled by Pennsylvania Dutch pushing down from the North and Scotch-Irish crossing
the mountains from Staunton. This was not the Promised Land as many
of them had expected, but it was a land of promise where towering
forests had never felt the bite of the axe and deep, rich soil had never
been broken by the blade of the plow. The land was not to be conquered
without heartbreak, misery, danger and death, but those who endured
the hardships inherited the land from the wilderness. The flow of settlers could not be stopped as they often planted their roots on land that
had been granted to a great landlord who was many miles and perhaps
even an ocean voyage away.

Wealthy and influential men to whom the Governor of Virginia
or King of England owed special favors gained the first titles to the
rich lands beyond the settlements. This was an assumption of ownership by proxy and in absentia that gave no consideration to the rights
of the red man who was often considered a wild animal and part of the
natural scene or to the common white settler hungry for land to call
his own.

Robert Green held the title to much of the land in present
Pendleton County. He divided his holdings into sections and sold the
large "upper tract" to William Shelton. This was the location of the

largest acreage of level bottom land in the present county and on the northern edge of which the town of Upper Tract is now situated. The Green grant was little more than a small plot of ground in comparison to the great Fairfax holdings.

The Fairfax grant had its beginning in 1649 when Charles II granted the land to followers of his father, Charles I, as a refuge when Cromwell came to power and took a rather dim view of the cavaliers who had been faithful to the elder Charles. All of this real estate dealing was going on in England with no one having taken a look at the property in question. The ownership of the land passed through a few heirs until it reached Thomas Lord Fairfax who came to America to see what Charles II had so graciously given the family. He built "Greenway Court" near Winchester and lived there the rest of his life overseeing the surveying and parcelling of his great land holdings. Lord Fairfax molded a warm friendship with young George Washington who surveyed for him throughout the area and also in the South Branch Valley.

The immediate item of business to be taken care of after the Lord arrived in America was the determination of the boundary of his holdings. The southern boundary was to be a line running from the first spring of the Potomac to the first spring of the Rappahannock. This was all well and good, but no one was sure of the location of the first spring of the Potomac. Lord Fairfax refused to approve the work of commissioners who first sought to determine the boundary and it was late in October 1746 when the Fairfax Stone was placed in position in present Tucker County at the headwaters of the North Branch of the Potomac River. Peter Jefferson, father of President Thomas Jefferson, was one of the surveyors involved in the determination of the Fairfax boundary. The Fairfax land which covered 2400 square miles became known as the "Northern Neck" and the Fairfax Stone has often been the deciding factor in disputes that have arisen between Virginia and Maryland over boundaries.

The wilderness was not a land of milk and honey, but rather a land of fur and feathers. Deer slipped silently through the forests and came warily to a spring or creek to drink. Bears lumbered through the woods and bear meat was eaten with as great a relish as was venison by the settlers. Even buffaloes and elk grazed beneath the trees in those early days to be followed by the prowling wolf pack or a mountain lion slipping through the shadows. Wild turkeys were abundant while eagles spread their pinions high over the craggy ridges. Valuable fur bearers such as the mink and beaver inhabited the streams and the forests where the crystal clear water along with the forest shade gave luster to their rich fur. The streams and rivers teemed with fish and to see a large trout break the surface must have been a common sight along the watercourses.

For a person familiar with the wildlife population of today which is only a segment of the number and variety found originally, it seems almost fantastic that large hoofed mammals such as the buffalo or woodland bison and elk once roamed much of the East. The bison is commonly associated with the plains where it supplied the horse Indians with sustenance, but it was found in the woodlands of the East as attested by the many places named for it which is also true in the case of the elk. Buffalo Hill near Franklin gets its name from the bison and Trout Run was formerly called Buffalo Run. The elk supplied a name for Elkhorn Mountain in Grant County.

The herds of bison and elk seem to have been most numerous along the valleys of the larger rivers and moved through the valleys and through mountain gaps that took them to winter feeding grounds or milder weather to the south. The last bison in West Virginia was killed at Valley Head, Randolph County, in 1825. The elk lingered for many years with a report of it near the headwaters of the Cheat River as late as 1873.

Wolves traveled in packs and this fact made them an even more frightening threat to the settlers. When snow lay deep upon the ground, settlers always avoided places where packs were known to roam. When the howl of the hungry pack came too close, the nearest escape route was up the closest big tree. Many tales are recorded of the hair-raising run-ins with wolf packs by settlers and there is little reason to doubt the validity of such stories. Wolves were enough of a threat to the settlers and their livestock that bounties were paid out for their scalps in many counties. Bounty hunting as well as outbreaks of hydrophobia within the packs put an end to the wolf in West Virginia by 1900.

The first county court in Pendleton County placed a one pound ($3.33) bounty on a grown wolf. The amount fluctuated over the years, but steadily grew larger. A. W. Roby killed two wolves in 1889 when the bounty payment had reached $35 for a single animal. Thomas A. Payne collected the same amount on one that he killed three years later. S. P. Dolly and Jacob Arbogast received the last payments made in the county when they killed two wolves in 1896, four years before the last known wolf in West Virginia was killed in nearby Randolph County.

The modern Vepco power plant on Stony River near Bismarck in Grant County is located on a site that was known as Wolf Rock. Until the plant was built, there was a rock outcropping extending for some distance along the ridge. Wolves found these rocks a haven where crevices ran several feet back underneath the rocks and earth offering shelter and dens to rear their young. The thick growth of laurel in the surrounding area made the place practically inpenetrable by hunters giving added refuge to the wolves. Zina Cosner recalls hearing his father tell of how the wolves would come from their dens in the rocks and gather into packs in the evening. Their howls filled the night air as they moved through the laurel and forests to prowl the countryside for food.

With the cutting of the forests in the 1880's, the wolves vacated their haunts at Wolf Rock and the last wolf in that part of Grant County was trapped by Jesse Cosner shortly after 1890. When the power plant was built, the rock was blasted and used in the fill of the dam. Few people who pass this way today would ever suspect that the site on which this modern electrical generating plant is located knew the tread of many wolves through possibly countless ages. The sight and sound of the animal that gave the now vanished rock its name lingers in the stories told by a few people who knew persons who had seen and heard the wolves of Wolf Rock.

About 1840, Martin Hamlin, a man reputed to have been of steel nerves and dead aim, went one evening to watch a deer lick on the west side of Stony River. In order to gain a good view of the place and to wait for the coming of the deer, he climbed into a large tree. After having made himself comfortable, he suddenly felt that he was not alone and saw a large mountain lion resting on a large limb and completely oblivious to his presence. The big cat was intently watching the ground and seemed to be there for the same purpose as Hamlin. Instead of shooting the panther and possibly spoiling his chances of getting a deer which might be quietly approaching the lick at that moment, Hamlin bided his time to see what developments would take place in this already odd situation. A large buck soon came to the lick, the panther plunged and killed the deer by breaking its neck. When the panther started to tear open the deer, Hamlin fired and both animals lay dead beneath the tree. With patience and resoluteness, Hamlin had brought down two trophies where, otherwise, he would have gotten only one.

Mountain lions usually hunted alone, but often one of the big cats was enough to make a settler's blood run cold. Bounties were paid out in some counties for the panther, particularly in the mountain counties where they were most common. Unlike many states in the East, West Virginia cannot show a date when its last mountain lion fell before a load of lead. It seemed to fade from the scene, but there are reliable reports of it being seen near Cranberry Glades as late as 1936. Like a ghost returning to haunt its tormentors, it may still be around if we put any faith in the many stories of recent sightings. Many years have passed and nothing real tangible has been caught to verify its presence, so maybe it is only a ghost.

Many old-timers will take you into their confidence and tell you of a time or two when they have seen the big cat, if they are sure they won't be ridiculed or the brunt of jokes as a result. Stories of strange tracks, a fleeting glimpse of a large, long-tailed cat and blood-chilling

screams are legion with hunters. While helping with the bird banding
at Red Creek a few years ago, Ralph Bell and I drove to the old Stony
River Dam to relieve the monotony of few birds to band and little to do.
The weather had gone foul with rain from time to time and fog rolling in
over the mountain. Before returning to the camp grounds, we drove to
the nearest town to find a store with a gas pump. A full tank of gas is
always good security from a long walk in this country.

While at the store, the conversation turned to the mounted bob-
cats with dusty fur and fixed snarls over the shelves of boxed and canned
goods. Someone dropped the question of the mountain lion into the conversation to which the storekeeper replied that he believes they are
still around. While deer hunting a few years before with friends near the
Stony River Dam, a loud scream, unlike any bobcat they had ever
heard, filled the air about dusk. He said, "I don't know what is was, but
it sure made the hair stand up on the back of your neck!" To this his
wife replied, "It didn't take you all long to get down off of that mountain either!"

Make of such stories what you will. One day you may see something that will convince you such stories are more than just imagination
and you will join the ranks of those who became firm believers long ago.
A bit of the grandeur of the past lingers in the tales that are told. Many
old-timers cling to the past by a thin thread in the stories they tell and
whether it is only a ghost or real flesh and blood fury remains to be
seen.

Many a Maryland hunter has read the story of the life of the
great hunter of western Maryland, Meshach Browning, with a feeling
of longing to return in time to join him in his pursuit of game when the
region was still a wilderness. Browning, whose life spanned the closing
years of the 18th Century and the first half of the 19th, lived in the area
of Cumberland in Allegany County. The stories he told of the number
of deer he killed as well as panthers, wolves and small game seem
almost unbelievable to the modern mind accustomed to fragmentary
game populations. Even though many people today may take rather
lightly some of his stories, the region was no doubt as heavily populated
with wildlife as the great hunter testified.

On at least two occasions Browning made trips with his sons up
the North Branch of the Potomac with the expressed purpose of finding
a place where no hunter had been before. After leaving their home, they
traveled for a day with a horse to carry supplies. After arriving in what
was then a part of Virginia, they found the hunting very good. Before
bedding down for the night, they shot a deer which eluded them and
seemingly escaped. They spent the night in a laurel thicket where they
had difficulty keeping the fire going and spent an uncomfortable night.
The following morning, the deer was found and they started home.

On a later trip made into the region, the elder Browning was separated from his sons and spent the night sleeping in a large hemlock. Snow was on the ground when he awoke the following morning, but all of his efforts and the uncomfortable night were not in vain when he killed a fine buck. His sons were attracted to him by the shot and the party was united. Browning laments that the trip was made as late in the year as it was because the deer and bears were leaving the woods of this cold and damp country as winter was near.

Today a big hunting party of several men and several dozen dogs hunt bears along the mountain around Dolly Sods. Blue Tick and Black and Tan hounds are most often used to hunt bear and a Black and Tan with a little Airedale in him makes a fine bear dog. A good 'coon hound can easily get the feel of trailing bears since the scent of a bear is said to be similar to that of the masked beggars he is used to chasing. Only a few of the best dogs will be lead into the woods to pick up the bear's trail and get the chase underway before the whole pack is turned loose to follow in howling pursuit.

The chase along the mountain may range over a mile or more. The bear can easily outdistance the dogs on a downhill run as it goes crashing through the brush and lumbering rapidly down the rocky slopes. On a steep, gradual climb the bear will begin to tire and the dogs can catch up and may even do battle with old bruin. While the chase is on and the reassuring howls of the hounds can be heard coming closer, the hunters have stationed themselves along the roads and trails from where they can get a shot at the bear when it crosses the road or comes into sight. No one may get the bear because it eluded the dogs and the hunters and is all tuckered, but miles away. For the real sportsman the day has not been a total loss because there has been the sport of the chase and knowing good dogs have done their best.

For the few hundred bears left in West Virginia it seems their days are numbered and they are living on borrowed time. The pressure from the growing number of hunters along with the bears killed out of season because they have supposedly been killing or molesting sheep will put an end to the bear in the Mountain State. It may not be long until the state mammal of West Virginia is not numbered among the fauna within its borders. Only strict hunting regulations and the stopping of out of season killing can perpetuate the black bear in West Virginia

Many changes have been wrought upon the land since the early days of settlement. Where the buffalo and elk once roamed, Hereford cattle peacefully graze as vultures rock lazily on the air currents. The turkey is found along the highest ridges where the last bears have joined them and now make their last stand against man and the movements of civilization. The howl of the wolf pack has long since become silent and only the ghost of the mountain lion lingers in the shadows. Only the deer remains of the wilderness mammals in enough numbers that they are hunted in the fall and can often be seen crossing a field during the day or by the highway at night.

When a fellow named Burner built his cabin in a clearing and became one of the first settlers in Pendleton County, deer were very numerous. From his doorstep, he could often watch a herd of about forty deer come to a stream to drink. Many years of unrestricted hunting nearly put an end to the deer in West Virginia by 1900. Since that time, hunting regulations and the stocking of deer from other states have brought them back. Some game management people in the state who should know insist that there are more deer in West Virginia today than when the first settlers arrived. The reasons are no competition from large hoofed mammals such as the buffalo and elk, practically no predators such as wolves and mountain lions and more open land for grazing today than originally.

Along with the large mammals that have been exterminated and have vanished from the region, it seems a few smaller mammals have disappeared or have been greatly reduced in numbers that were once found here. A relative of the mink which may have at one time been a member of the fauna of the region is the fisher. Due to its rather robust appearance and superficial resemblance to a fox, this animal was often called the "black fox." While a mammal of the North Woods of Canada, it seems that at one time the range of the fisher extended along the mountains as far south as North Carolina. The records of the fisher in West Virginia are scant and while there are no known records for the upper Potomac region, formerly the mammal may have been found at least rarely in the spruce along the higher elevations. Thaddeus Surber reported in a list of mammals that he compiled many years ago that the fisher was once found in the spruce belt along the high mountains.

The last known record for this member of the weasel family in West Virginia was made during the early 1870's. A pelt that turned up at a St. Louis fur dealer in 1939 proved to be that of a fisher and it was traced back to Gilmer County. Whether the fisher had been in that part of the state all along or this animal had wandered into that area from farther north still poses a mystery.

While the evidence is scant, it seems that the porcupine was formerly found in Pendleton County. Years ago there were reports that from time to time one was killed in the pine forests on the slopes of Spruce Mountain.

Another species of mammal that has a rather uncertain status within the region is the spotted skunk. Three decades ago, there were many reports from trappers that the spotted skunk was found in some numbers along the South Branch River and some authorities reported seeing pelts of this mammal in stores in Franklin. If the spotted skunk is around it has succeeded in eluding me. The examination of many smelly road kills has failed to turn up a spotted skunk and all have proved to be the remains of the common and widespread striped skunk.

The bobcat continues to hold out in the mountain fastness where they often make their dens around rocky ledges. On occasions one of them crosses the path of a hunter and ends up adorning a den or a trophy case in the hunter's home. Stanley Hedrick of Upper Tract tells the story that while squirrel hunting on Cave Mountain a few years ago, a bobcat approached him. The cat was walking down a path towards him and seemed oblivious to his presence, but uncertain as to whether or not the cat simply did not see him or was mad or rabid as it came at him, he took no chances and fired his shotgun into the cat's face. The bobcat wheeled and ran several yards before dropping dead. The outcome of all of this can be seen in the mounted bobcat that is now found in the Hedrick home.

No consideration of the mammals that were found in the region formerly or even today would be complete without some mention of the beaver. In many respects this big rodent was responsible for the exploration of the West when fortunes were made almost overnight and lost just as fast when beaver hats were in vogue during the early years of the 19th Century.

The beaver was found throughout the state at the time of settlement and Daniel Boone trapped them in the Kanawha Valley, but the demands for its pelt and the onrush of civilization exterminated the beaver in West Virginia before the turn of the century. For many years there were no reports of it in the state and no one seemed to know where any of them could be found even if they held on in the mountains somewhere. Since then they have made a comeback either through restocking or by moving into the state from elsewhere. Today they are found on the Roaring Plains along Allegheny Front and they have built dams and created ponds on Dickinson Mountain not far from Franklin. When a person is patient in his vigil at one of these ponds, he may see one of the beavers swimming or hear it slapping the water with its flat tail.

While a number of the larger mammals once found in the region have disappeared and some of the smaller ones have an uncertain status today, there are many mammals that are found as rather widespread and even numerous. It is not an uncommon sight to see the fox squirrel in the woodlots, along a rail fence and in the forests throughout the region. The large rufous-furred squirrel seems to be rather numerous. One day in early March, a squirrel ran across the road in front of the car near Brushy Run and while I at first thought it was a large gray squirrel, then I realized it was the melanistic or black phase of the

Fig. 1. The raccoon will most often be seen during the hours of darkness when 'coon hunters and their hounds make it the object of their pursuits or it comes sniffing around a campsite in search of scraps to eat.

fox squirrel. It was black about the head, very dark along its body, but there were a few telltale rufous hairs in the tail. I was suprised to see this squirrel and considered myself fortunate to have seen a black fox squirrel, but on a recent visit to the taxidermy shop of Marvin Rexrode at Fort Seybert, I saw two melanistic fox squirrels that he had mounted and which had been shot locally. It seems that black fox squirrels are not very unusual in the area and turn up on occasions in the sights of hunters.

The little red squirrel which is often dubbed "fairydiddle" by hunters is a resident of the spruce and hemlock forests at the higher elevations, but it is not uncommon to find this squirrel in a variety of situations at lower elevations. The large white pines in the cemetery at Franklin offer the red squirrel a haven and they can often be seen and heard calling their buzzing chatter there. They often find the towns to their liking and they have been seen in the shade trees in Upper Tract.

Along the highways after dark is a good place to see mammals abroad. One evening in early September while driving from Moorefield, the headlights of my car shone on the backs of three forms that were crossing the road. I put on the brakes because when I had first seen these forms, I thought they were sheep. After they had crossed the highway and one crouched by the road, it was then that I realized they were raccoons and the three largest raccoons I have ever seen.

While I saw these three raccoons on the highway, anyone who camps knows that it may not be long before he will have masked visitors as they come sniffing around a campsite or rustling through garbage to find scraps to eat. If anyone is a real fancier of raccoons, then he should join a party of 'coon hunters and before the night is over, while he may be worn out from chasing the howling hounds across the country-side, he will usually get to see at least one, if not several, 'coons up a tree. For the person who prefers to have his observations of wildlife made under less strenuous circumstances and without the thrill of the chase, he may find himself a campsite along a stream, throw out a few scraps and wait for the beggars of night to come to him.

After dark one may get a fleeting glimpse of a red fox as it flashes across the pavement in front of the revealing headlights of a car. Cottontails are seen commonly along the road as they bound away with their puff of a tail flashing. Skunks and the dim-witted opossum are frequently caught by the lights of a car as they forage for food and often come to grief with a car on the highway.

The high elevations along Spruce Mountain and the Allegheny Front offer environmental conditions for mammals which are found at few places in the state and might be considered more characteristically mammals of the North. One of these is the snowshoe hare or varying hare, a relative of the cottontail that is brown throughout most of the year, but assumes white fur during the winter months. During 1936 when a party of collectors from the National Museum was collecting mammals in West Virginia, it seems that the snowshoe hare was at a low population ebb and its numbers had been greatly reduced by an epidemic that periodically strikes the species. A. B. Brooks lists the snowshoe hare as a resident of the spruce and mixed hardwood forests on Spruce Mountain when he was carrying on field work there during June of 1908. This hare which is a common species in Canadian and boreal zones along the high Appalachians, no doubt finds a number of suitable places at the high elevations along the western edge of the region where the landscape and the plant life are so strikingly similar to its haunts in Canada.

Among the small, obscure and rarely seen mammals of the high elevations is the smoky shrew, a resident of the floor of the spruce forest, bogs and stream banks. A northern form of the white-footed mouse, of which there are several species, is often found around rocky places and it was in such situations that the Smithsonian collectors were able to secure a number of specimens near Spruce Knob. The red-backed mouse is a resident of the floor of the forest where it often makes its burrows under the moss and near the roots of spruce and yellow birch, but this species is not confined to the spruce country since it occurs in a number of other situations at lower elevations within the state. The interesting star-nosed mole which has acquired its name from the odd looking rays of flesh on its snout and which serve about the same purpose as a blind man's cane has been found in Pendleton County where one was collected by Fred Brooks on Big Run during the summer of 1908.

This has been a close look at the land that can be encompassed in the view from Shenandoah and the events that have played a part in making it what it is today. The wilderness in its magnificent and forbidding nature has long since fallen before the march of civilization and only its last, fading days linger in the memories of a few very old people. For the person who seeks to know more fully the wild inhabitants of the land, there are adventures ahead that will bring him in faint touch with the mood of the wilderness which one may seek to recapture, but which is now gone forever in its fullest grandeur.

CHAPTER TWO

THE STORY IN THE ROCK

As I have stood looking up at the nearly 1000 foot high gray face of Seneca Rocks, I have wondered what impressions this widely known and much photographed sight has made upon the many people who have chanced to pass this way. The tourist from out of state may hastily snap a picture or two while thinking it is time to be on the road again in order to reach Blackwater Falls or some other prime tourist attraction, before the light becomes too dim for photography. The mountain climbing enthusiast may look up with eager anticipation of the adventure that lies ahead as he practices his skill with ropes on a steeplejack hike up the front. The person fascinated by wide vistas will attempt the less treacherous climb up the back for a view up and down the valley from its lofty crest. The local people who have lived their lives in the shadow of the mighty rocks may only find it an eternal landmark that was there long before they were born and will continue to stand long after they are gone. To the businesses of the area this act of nature means money in their pockets from the tourists who come to look and use the gas stations, motels and restaurants.

How many people in the fleeting minutes or hours they may spend within sight of Seneca Rocks grasp fully the grandeur of this sight? How many of them have some inkling of the forces that were at work during countless ages through the vast sweep of immeasurable time to sculpture this wonder in stone? To fully appreciate and understand the magnificence of Seneca Rocks, one must know something of its origin as a result of geological processes.

When one begins to grasp the age of the cliffs and the remarkable forces of compression and upheaval that went into their making, suddenly his hurried life becomes as nothing before the unhurried ages that shaped and molded the rocks into their present form. For the person who looks up in reverence with thoughts that plumb the depths of his mind for a comprehension of the age of the earth, he will find himself involved in thoughts that border on the contemplation of eternity.

Countless ages compressed into a few moments of thought reveal a shallow sea into which sediments were deposited followed by the vast flow of time until the Appalachians were thrust from the earth only to be eroded to their present form and then one's thoughts are resting again upon the present. Such a momentary journey through the ages may lead one to seek more about the origin of the mountains and valleys and the cliffs and caves. What began as casual contemplation may become a burning interest that leads one to become an amateur geologist with rock hammer in hand or a spelunker with a head lamp on his hat.

Our story in stone is now underway and with Seneca Rocks as our starting point, we will begin our journey through the valleys and across the mountains with frequent lapses into the depths of time to piece together the puzzle whose pieces are scattered all about us, but the key to which lies in the past. From Seneca Rocks our trip through distance and time will take us to other outstanding geological formations in the region for a study of their origin and the addition of other pieces to the mosaic we know as the land forms and the rock formations of the upper Potomac highlands.

From Seneca Rocks we will follow U.S. route 33 southward to Judy Gap and drive up the slope of the mountain to the overlook where we can look across Germany Valley. Germany Valley is without a doubt one of the most beautiful valleys in West Virginia and the view from route 33 ranks as one of the most beautiful in the entire Appalachian Mountain region.

As we look down into the depths of the valley, we see the many farms with their pasture land and woodlots spread across the length of the valley as we look northward towards the northern end of Pendleton County. In the floor of the valley there are rich deposits of limestone and the limestone that is quarried there by the Greer Limestone Company is almost pure calcium carbonate. We also know that the valley is underlain by limestone because here is located Seneca Caverns, Stratosphere Balloon Cave which was operated commercially for many years before it was closed some years ago to the public, Schoolhouse Cave which has been dubbed the "toughest cave in America" for exploration and another widely known cave that proves the skill of spelunkers which is Hellhole Cave.

We can find evidence of the limestone even if we know nothing of the caves that are beneath the floor of the valley or the quarry operation of the Greer Company through the richness of the soil, the lush grass and the prosperous farms located in the valley. This all stems from the fact that the vegetation is fed by rich limestone soil.

Up the mountain slope above the floor of the valley, we find outcroppings of rock which can be seen along the highway near the over-

Fig. 2. Imposing landmark at Mouth of Seneca and the inspiration for legends, the Tuscarora sandstone cliffs of Seneca Rocks are the most widely known geological formation at the headwaters of the Potomac River.

look. These rocks date from a later time in geological history than the limestone found in the valley. Near the overlook and on up the mountain along the highway, we find sandstones that are brown or reddish in color. At a number of places the strata is rich with the fossils of shelled organisms that lived in the sea ages ago.

As we look eastward and lift our sights a little higher, we see along the crest of the mountain the high cliffs that cap the top of North Fork Mountain and run for many miles through Pendleton County and on into Grant County. These cliffs are the Tuscarora sandstone that also forms Seneca Rocks. Formerly, among geologists and in the literature in the field, this sandstone was called the White Medina, but Tuscarora is widely used today when reference is made to it.

Looking westward across the valley, we see a number of knobby mountains that are capped with rock strata standing on end. Here again we have the Tuscarora sandstone, the same sandstone we find along the top of North Fork Mountain. Ages ago, the sandstone along the River Knobs between the North Fork River and Germany Valley was continuous with the sandstone that caps the top of the mountain. In ages that have elapsed since, great pressure was exerted on the Tuscarora sandstone that caused it to be uplifted and the rock strata that was found from the top of the mountain to the River Knobs has been removed by erosion.

As we look beyond the River Knobs, we see the lofty ridge of Spruce Mountain where the highest point at Spruce Knob at 4860 feet is the highest point in West Virginia. Beyond Spruce Mountain lies Allegheny Mountain and as one drives west from Mouth of Seneca towards Onego and on to Harman, he will cross the steep front of this mountain. Allegheny Mountain serves as a secondary continental divide within the United States. The streams that flow on the western side of the mountain eventually drain into the Ohio and Mississippi and into the Gulf of Mexico. The streams on the eastern slopes of the mountain flow into the branches of the Potomac and find their outlet into the Chesapeake Bay and into the Atlantic Ocean.

By highway 28 as one drives from Pendleton County into Pocahontas County, there is a marker that calls that area the "birthplace of rivers." One crosses Allegheny Mountain just beyond that point and near there the Cheat River heads up and flows north while the Greenbrier has its start in a mountain swamp and flows south. East of this point, the branches of the Potomac begin their northward flow while the head streams of the James River trickle south. There is a story told that near Monterey there is a barn that sits on the divide between the watersheds of the Potomac and James. When it rains, the water running down one side of the roof finds its way into the Potomac and the water dripping off the other side of the barn runs into the headwaters of the James or so the story goes.

As we stand at the overlook viewing the valley and knowing from the rich soil and caves that there is limestone beneath the ground and as we look at the strata higher up along the mountain where the Tuscarora sandstone outcrops to form high cliffs, we will turn our attention to the forces necessary for the formation of the valley and many of the other outstanding geological features in the region. This calls for some imagination, some speculation and the consideration of tremendous periods of time that went into the laying down of the rock strata that eventually formed Seneca Rocks, Germany Valley, North Fork Mountain, Spruce Mountain and many of the other prominent features that have an important place in any consideration of the geology of the upper Potomac.

We all know scientists are prone to catalogue and classify things and geologists are no exception. Classification is necessary for convenience and ease in communication when talking about a particular thing. Geologists have divided the vast sweep of the earth's formation into various eras and periods for convenient reference points. Such a system of classification is based upon the appearance of certain characteristic plant and animal forms or certain geological events at particular times through the myriad ages that have passed during the ebb and flow of events on the face of our planet.

The Paleozoic Era is a great segment of geological time that includes all of the ebb and flow of events on the face of the earth from about 600 million to about 230 million years ago. This great block of earth history is further divided into a number of periods. The first period of the Paleozoic is the Cambrian and it was during this long span of earth time that the first recognizable forms of life that have been preserved as fossils made their appearance. When geologists plumb the depths of the rocks that were formed before this time, there is no direct evidence of life forms. The only place in West Virginia where conditions have brought about the exposure of Cambrian strata is in Berkeley and Jefferson Counties. Throughout the rest of the state, these rocks are buried far below younger strata.

The limestone quarried in Germany Valley was formed from limy sediments laid down during the Ordovician period. We have now entered the period that is estimated to have lasted for 75 million years following the close of the Cambrian. Geologists believe that during this time much of the present land area of the United States was covered by shallow seas which were connected with the oceans. The shallow sea that covered the present Appalachian region was probably bordered at a number of points by land areas. Do not think that the surface of the earth was anything like the earth as we know it today. Much of the surface of the earth at this time was beneath the sea and life had not made its appearance on land. The sediments that were laid down in this shallow sea were limy sediments from the bodies of marine organisms and shelled creatures that lived in the sea.

The question might naturally arise as to how geologists know that the region was beneath a shallow sea. When a sea is fairly shallow and the land masses in the process of erosion are some distance away, the strata most likely to be formed is limestone from the calcium contained in the bodies of marine organisms. These were the circumstances that lead to the laying down of beds of limestone at various times during geological history. When sand, silt and clay have been deposited, this means that the land from which this material has been eroded was fairly close to the area of deposition. From these understandings of the processes necessary for the formation of sedimentary rocks, geologists can gain something of a picture of the earth's surface in the remote past.

Let us imagine, in considering this sea, a trough that was a few hundred miles wide by several hundred miles long which covered much of what we know today as the mid-Appalachian region. Into this trough various sediments were being deposited along with the calcium from marine life. These sediments came from land areas that surrounded this trough which has been called the Appalachian geosyncline which means a great depression in the crust of the earth. The geosyncline seems to have been shallower along its western edge than to the east where the greatest amount of sediment accumulated and where the crust of the earth yielded to the weight of these sediments through subsidence.

Throughout the Silurian which began a little over 400 million years ago and lasted 20 million years, we find that the sea continued to ebb and flow across much of the area we know as the Alleghenies. It was during the Silurian period that the Tuscarora sandstone that forms Seneca Rocks had its beginning in sediments that were washed into the bed of the sea.

In dealing with the Silurian, mention must be made of the exposures of igneous rocks that are found in conjunction with Silurian strata in Pendleton County where the only known exposures of rocks of volcanic origin in West Virginia are found. As one drives southward along Shenandoah Mountain from Reddish Knob and begins the descent of the mountain slope, he will come to a Forest Service sign that calls one's attention to the fact that the rocks here are igneous. The rock here is a slate-blue in color when it is fractured to expose its color. Until several years ago, the only known igneous rock in Pendleton County was located south of Sugar Grove about a half-mile from the Virginia line where it was exposed over an area about 200 by 500 feet. Since that time, investigations on the part of geology students from West Virginia University and members of the W. Va. Geological Survey have found a number of other igneous exposures in southeastern Pendleton County.

The first known exposure of this rock that was molded by great heat and pressure presented something of a geological mystery since it is surrounded by outcroppings of Silurian age up through which it must have been forced. Recent investigations would seem to indicate that the igneous rocks have been deposited as a result of its intruding into and cutting through the associated Silurian strata during the more recent Triassic period. Whatever the answer may be, the few known exposures of igneous rocks in West Virginia are quite out of step with the processes of sea, sand and sediment that formed the strata throughout the state.

Before leaving the Silurian and turning to the following period of the Devonian, mention must be made of the Lost River Sinks between Baker and Wardensville in Hardy County near highway 259. The Tonoloway limestone through which Lost River has cut its way underground lies at the very top of the Silurian system and beneath the base of the Helderberg series of the overlying Devonian. The water flows underground for two miles beneath Sandy Ridge before it emerges to form the Cacapon River.

During the Devonian there continued to be the laying down of sediments in the bed of the sea. With the end of this period, there was

Fig. 3. View of the back of Eagle Rock with Oriskany sandstone cliffs on Cave Mountain beyond. These and other resistant strata from the Devonian that outcrop dramatically along the South Branch River near this point have given the Smoke Hole country much of its rugged character.

a withdrawal of the sea from what is now the present state of West Virginia as well as surrounding areas. The sediments deposited during this time were to play a great part in the formation of the limestone and sandstones of the Helderberg and Oriskany series that outcrop at a number of places in the Pendleton, Grant and Hardy area. At Petersburg Gap these formations have been exposed in sheer cliffs along both sides of the river before they dip out of sight near where the bridge is located. As one drives towards Moorefield, the Oriskany sandstone has been exposed in spectacular cliffs with Baker Rock being most easily seen from the main highway. South along the mountain from Baker Rock, other jagged palisades of this sandstone almost have the appearance of a fortress wall built by giants. Another outstanding example of the Oriskany sandstone is the steeply tilted strata of Eagle Rock in the Smoke Hole near Upper Tract.

By looking at Germany Valley, we see that the youngest strata near the valley is the Tuscarora sandstone. The Devonian with its sandstones and shales is younger and is not in evidence in Germany Valley or along North Fork Mountain due to the fact that the overlying Devonian rock has been removed through erosion. Devonian strata lies to the east of the valley at such points as in the Smoke Hole and also to the west along the North Fork River in the neighborhood of Riverton.

The Devonian is especially important to the scientist who studies fossil plants, a paleobotanist, because the first forests made their appearance on land during this period. The Devonian forests were far different from the familiar forests of today with the trees of those forests being large plants similar to the ferns and club mosses with which everyone who tramps the forest is familiar. The tallest "tree" may have reached a height of thirty feet and were much smaller in size than the enormous plants that were to grow later in the forests of the Coal Age or even the forests of today. Even though these first trees were small in size and strange in comparison to the trees we know today, a great advance had been made in the plant world. Plants had taken the first giant step in lifting their heads far above the ground to create the forests that give man many raw materials to sustain his life and without which our world would be a bleak and barren place.

The Mississippian dawned with the closing days of the Devonian and this period of earth history began about 340 million years ago and lasted for some odd 30 million years. During this period, much of the present state of West Virginia and surrounding areas were again beneath the sea. The thick beds of Greenbrier limestone that are found at a number of places in the state lend evidence to the fact that much of the Allegheny region was under the waters of a sea. During this time, we find that fish began to make their appearance in numbers in the sea, but they were far different in structure from the fish that we are familiar with today and were more closely related to the sharks and such fresh-water oddities as the sturgeon. The land above water was covered by forests very similar to the Devonian forests and the early air-breathing vertebrates lived on land and looked like giant versions of the salamanders.

The outstanding feature from the Mississippian that is found in the three county area is Helmick Rock on South Branch Mountain above the South Fork River not far from Moorefield. The Pocono sandstone that is exposed here in high cliffs dates from the base of the Mississippian period. From a number of high points in Hardy and its neighbor counties, it is possible to see the prominent feature of Helmick Rock where the Pocono sandstone ends abruptly in cliffs on the mountain crest.

The Mississippian and the following period, the Pennsylvanian, are often lumped together and called the Carboniferous in reference to the vast deposits of coal that had their initial formation during these periods. During the Pennsylvanian, most of the land area of the region

Fig. 4. Spruce Knob in Pendleton County where the highest point in West Virginia is located. The Pottsville conglomerate exposed here that dates from the Pennsylvanian is the youngest rock in the county. The rigorous weather conditions at this high elevation are apparent from the sparse vegetation.

was again above water. The climate was warm throughout the year and the land was covered by vast forests of vegetation very similar to the ferns, club mosses and horsetails that are often found growing in damp places in the forests today. These plants grew to tree size in those ages long ago and as this vegetation died and its decay was retarded by the dampness of the earth or by being covered by other vegetation, the process began that through pressure over great lengths of time lead to the formation of the coal that is mined so many places in West Virginia and neighboring states.

The youngest rock in Pendleton County is the Pottsville conglomerate found at Spruce Knob which is coarsely grained and studded with white pebbles. The exposed strata down the slopes of Spruce Mountain from the knob date from the Mississippian and are older. The Pottsville conglomerate is found along the escarpment of Allegheny Front in Grant County where it forms such prominent features as Bear Rocks and other cliffs along the edge of the Roaring Plains. When one thinks of the Pennsylvanian period, they usually think of coal and in the three county area coal is found beyond the Allegheny Front in northwestern Grant County where it is strip mined to feed the hungry Vepco plant.

Let us again turn our thoughts to the formation of Germany Valley. As vast lengths of time passed during the various periods of the Paleozoic Era when much of Appalachia was covered by a sea, the surface of the earth was sinking due to the weight of the sediment that was being washed into the trough of the Appalachian geosyncline. It was towards the end of the Paleozoic that crustal disturbances occurred that were to bring about the uplifting of the Appalachian Mountains.

Formerly, much attention was focused on the Permian period as the time when the initial phases of mountain building took place, but recent investigations would seem to reveal that the process of crustal uplift was not limited to this period of the Paleozoic and no doubt began in pre-Permian times. As geologists have studied fossil evidence from the Permian as it is found at various places in the United States and throughout the world, it seems that this was a time when the earth underwent a number of changes. The climate became much drier and reptiles began to make their appearance upon the face of the earth which was to lead to the emergence of the dinosaurs in a whole host of forms and varieties.

The process of mountain building had its beginning in a great force that was exerted, a driving force of tremendous proportions that completely staggers the human imagination. This force seems to have been exerted from the area that we know today as southeastern Virginia and was driving westward. The many thousands of feet of sediment that had been deposited into the Appalachian geosyncline began to emerge in the formation of mountain ridges and valleys.

Germany Valley seems an open book to an understanding of this great driving force and the processes that were involved in buckling the earth's surface with the result that the strata became elevated to form the valley that we know today. Here we see that the Tuscarora sandstone was once continuous from the top of North Fork Mountain to the River Knobs. Ages ago these strata were horizontal and as this great driving force was exerted northwestward, the sandstone was forced to bow upward. As ages of erosion occurred, the sandstone from the top of the mountain to the knobs was washed away. The force that was necessary to stand these monolithic layers of sandstone on their end is beyond imagination, but when we consider the time necessary for their formation our minds are strained. The lofty outcroppings of this sandstone that runs for many miles along the mountain ridges have often made me think of the fins on the back of some slumbering giant from the days of the dinosaurs.

When a person tries to picture the Tuscarora sandstone continuously from the top of the mountain to the River Knobs, he can imagine a great wave breaking along the seashore. The slope along the eastern side of North Fork Mountain is not an especially steep slope and is

Fig. 5. View northward towards North Fork Gap along the crest of North Fork Mountain. The Allegheny Front is in the left distance beyond the valley of the North Fork River. This is a good point from which to view the outcroppings of Tuscarora sandstone.

rather gentle in places. At the top of the mountain, the sandstone arches and drops sharply at the knobs like a great wave breaking upon the shore. When the sandstone from the Silurian was removed through erosion, the underlying rocks from the Ordovician were exposed. The great force that lead to the formation of the mountains and valleys of the region may have been in operation over vast periods of time since it seems that the Appalachians have been uplifted and worn down more than once. The forces of uplift and erosion have been at odds during vast segments of time as the surface of the earth has been driven into folds only to have the mountains removed through the agents of water, wind, freezing and thawing.

We will now turn our attention to the way in which the rivers have played a role in eroding the rock strata and forming the present land surface and topography that we find in the upper Potomac country. A number of factors are involved here, but it seems that in some cases the rivers have followed their present courses for many millions of years. There is evidence to support the view that the uplift of the strata occurred as the rivers continued to maintain their ancient courses. The rocks were being uplifted so slowly and imperceptibly through great lengths of time that the streams were able to carry on their work of erosion and maintain their courses.

Along New Creek Mountain, Kline, Cosner and Greenland Gaps would offer evidence that as the mountain was being uplifted the streams that flow through the gaps were able to cut their courses at right angle to the axis of the ridge. North Fork Gap where the North Fork River flows through the divide between North Fork and New Creek Mountains would offer similar evidence. While many of the rivers and streams in the region have cut their way downward through less resistant rock to form the trellised stream pattern where the streams run parallel to the mountain ridges, it would also seem that at various places the streams have maintained their courses as the land was uplifted along their courses and their banks grew higher with the passing ages.

As we stand at the overlook on U.S. route 33 looking across Germany Valley, it is time to turn our attention to one of the most interesting aspects of the geology of the region which is the limestone caves. Many people come each year to explore the caves in Pendleton and neighboring counties from the various Grottos of the National Speleological Society in many of the larger cities not far from the region. In recent years, so many of them have come that they have what could be called a caver's convention when they pitch their tents at McCoy's Mill south of Franklin or at other camping areas in the county before they fan out across the countryside to search out and enjoy the underground scenery of the area.

Pendleton County falls into third place among the counties in the state having the largest number of caves. Greenbrier County tops the list with over a hundred known caves within its limestone rich boundaries. Pocahontas County is second with some seventy odd caves while Pendleton County is third, but running Pocahontas a close race for second, with sixty odd known caves. Caving is one of the few areas of endeavor where there is still an opportunity for real discovery since there are doubtless a number of caves in Pendleton County and other counties that have yet to be discovered and described. During the decade following 1950, nearly a dozen new and hitherto unknown caves were located and described in Pendleton County. So it is indeed possible for the conscientious spelunker not only to add a great deal of information to our knowledge about known caves, but even to chance across in some little known and out of the way place the entrance to a cave that has never been brightened by the probing beam from a spelunker's lamp.

Nearly a dozen caves are found under the limestone rich sod in Germany Valley and this is a good place to begin our speleological expedition to a number of the caves in the county where we will consider their interesting aspects of geology, limestone formations and history. For one who has never been underground or tried the fine art of spelunking, Seneca Caverns seems a good place to begin because the only equipment one needs to go caving in the Caverns is the money

Fig. 6. Germany Valley under a blanket of snow. Few areas reveal as many aspects of the geology of the region as does the valley and its environs. The valley is a mecca for spelunkers since some of the most challenging caves in the region are located here.

for admission. In order to get the feel of the underground world of caves, we will drive into the valley and take the guided tour through Seneca Caverns.

The guide informs us that a dozen million years ago the caverns were an underground river. This would seem another way of saying that for an extremely long period of time great volumes of water were at work here enlarging the passageways and rooms where the tourist now trods. The volume of water was greater than the deposition of calcium leached from the limestone and the process of enlargement went on for a very long time. Only when the water failed to enter the caverns in torrents did the formations have their beginnings. As the water percolated through the limestone, slowly it began to work the wonders that are now a part of the caverns. For endless years, endless drops of water carrying a small load of calcium from the limestone worked to the surface where they evaporated, but left in their stead the calcium that meant the birth of a stalactite.

Through countless ages, the water and limestone joined in a partnership of chemical processes that laid the foundation and built the variety of formations that are found in Seneca Caverns. The wonders in stone were hidden within the darkness of the earth as the processes of their creation went on as it does today. Legend has it that the Indians were the first men to wander into the depths of the caverns. In more recent times, a fellow named Teter chanced onto his only claim to any fame when he discovered the caverns about 1780 or rediscovered them if we want to give the Indians any credit. The gingle of coins was not heard at the mouth of the caverns until 1930 when they were commercialized.

A large flowstone mound called the Dutch Oven is located near the entrance which is made through a shallow sink. This formation, so aptly named, was formed by layers of the flowstone material being laid down until the mound reached its present height and circumference at the base of about fifty-five feet.

In the Ballroom, a room about sixty feet long by thirty feet wide, there is a model pyramid and a formation called the Tower of Pisa, part of which now lies prostrate on the floor. On the wall above the Pyramid can clearly be seen the place where this rock once reposed until it was shaken loose. The tower was also shaken at the same time and lost its top. Ages ago, some quarter of a million years the guide says, the earth shifted. During the stirring of the strata, the Pyramid found its way to the floor and the tower was fractured never to grow again. When this occurred, the movement of moisture over the tower stopped and it now leans as any replica of the Tower of Pisa should lean, but it will never rise beyond its present height. It knew a grander day long ago and now the process of deterioration goes on within its columned structure.

An alcove called the Balcony is suspended from the ceiling beyond the Ballroom. The Balcony takes on a warm atmosphere with the use of light to accentuate a thin stalagmite that serves as a candlestick and a recess called the fireplace. Along the wall at the end of the Ballroom, there is a large flowstone formation which is capped by the Capitol Dome and known as Candy Mountain. This formation is still growing and its frosty look added to the beauty of its rich blue-gray, milk shake brown and cream colors that ripple downward towards its base and along its icy fingers.

Just beyond Candy Mountain is the Balanced Rock which was rended from the overhanging wall at the same time as the Tower of Pisa received its death blow. The steps lead downward to a point where the Balanced Rock is overhead and to the lowest point in the caverns which is 165 feet below the ground with the ceiling overhead sixty-five feet high. From this low point, one works his way up to where he was formerly.

Near this point on the tour, an area is called the Council Room and is reputed to have been the place where Chief Bald Eagle of the Senecas met with the sages of his tribe. Years ago tomahawks and arrow points were found near this point in the caverns. If the Indians did enter the dark depths of the caverns where they no doubt believed that demons dwelt, it was more likely to quarry the formations for use in making pipes and ornaments than to sit around and make tribal decisions.

Snow Bird, the daughter of Bald Eagle, is enshrined forever in the caverns. The fame of Snow Bird extends to Seneca Rocks where, as a child, she scaled the precipitous heights and performed a feat that had never been accomplished. She used this test of strength and courage on a number of would-be suitors by climbing to the heights and deeming the one who reached her first as her future husband. Near the entrance to the caverns, a profile on the wall can easily be likened to that of a woman. This could be the profile of any woman who might come to mind, but since the legend of Snow Bird is such a part of the story of the caverns and Seneca Rocks then I suppose it is fitting that her Indian features should be seen in the formation.

Until the caverns were developed commercially, the Council Room was the farthest point that a person could reach. It was necessary to enlarge the passageways beyond this point before the area beyond could become part of the tour. Along the man-made passageway lies Fairy Land, the fastest growing area in the caverns and a fact betrayed by the dripping of water. An infinite number of pencil-sized stalactites hang from the ceiling of Fairy Land and are on their way to meet their counterparts growing from the floor. Rimstone pools nearby have worked into a relief that looks very much like the borders of the continental United States.

As we step outside into the daylight, the air will seem much warmer than it did before we entered the caverns. The air temperature inside hovers around 54°F at all seasons of the year and this explains the feeling of sudden warmth outside. If a person spent some time in the frigid air of winter, entering the caverns would have the opposite effect and he would welcome what seemed a warm underground world.

The people who tend the cash registers, curio shops and guide the tours at the commercial caverns may become impatient with me when I hack away at the legends and the likenesses of various things as seen in the variety of formations. I am a person who believes that the legends and likenesses are really quite unnecessary since the beauty of the formations speak for themselves. I know my time has not been wasted and my money well spent when I look at the wonders that have been wrought by water and stone. All that one sees underground had its beginning before the things we liken them to. Before there was an architect, the Tower of Pisa and a pyramid were underground in what is now Seneca Caverns. Possibly even before there was a woman, the likeness of Snow Bird was etched on that cavern wall. These are the

Fig. 7. A large flowstone formation near the entrance of Stratosphere Balloon Cave. One of the oldest known caves in the region, it has a number of large and interesting formations and was once operated commercially.

things that make a journey underground meaningful because one sees creation at work where time becomes as nothing and a thousand years can be spent in laying a foundation and a million spent in raising a column.

One of the oldest known caves in the region is Stratosphere Balloon which was formerly called Asbury Cave after Bishop Francis Asbury of the Methodist Church who, tradition holds, visited the cave in 1781 during one of his evangelical expeditions through the area. The notes that are recorded in his Journal would leave little doubt that this is the cave he entered unless he visited Seneca Caverns.

During the latter part of June, 1781, Asbury entered Germany Valley and speaks of the difficulty of crossing North Fork Mountain. He preached to about ninety "Dutch folk" who, in his own words, "appeared to feel the word." He also describes the large spring found in the valley. As a diversion from evangelism, he went spelunking on Wednesday, June 21, 1781. He writes in his Journal:

Last evening I rode a mile and a half to see some of the greatest natural curiosities my eyes ever beheld--they were two caves about

two hundred yards from each other: their entrances were, in similar cases, narrow and descending, gradually widening towards the interior, and opening into lofty chambers, supported, to appearance, by basaltic pillars: in one of these I sung,
"Still out of the deepest abyss, "
The sound was wonderful. There were stalactites resembling the pipes of an organ, which when our guide, father Ellsworth, struck with a stick, emitted a melodious sound, with variations according to their size: walls, like our old churches; resemblances to the towers adjoining their belfries; and the natural gallery, which we ascended with difficulty--all to me was new, solemn, and awfully grand.--There were parts which we did not explore--so deep, so damp, and near night.--I came away filled with wonder, with humble praise, and adoration.

The entrance to Stratosphere Balloon Cave lies at the bottom of a shallow sink about twenty feet deep. The weather beaten steps from the days when the cave was operated commercially were descended cautiously to the lattice work door which I felt was so reminiscent of the door of a dungeon. I passed the key to Linton Sites, the lock snapped open and we were standing in the near darkness behind the door. The carbide lantern and head lamps were lighted and the formations and features near the entrance began to appear out of the darkness. Here were a number of flowstone formations along the walls which seemed to have long since ceased growing. They were dull and deteriorated except for some recent growth on a few which may have begun recently or may have been due to seasonal movements of moisture.

Not far from the entrance lies the moment of decision where there are two passageways with one to the left and another to the right. The one to the left continues for a short distance before it comes to an end. The one to the right becomes spacious as the descent begins through the cave and finally to the Stratosphere Balloon formation as its climax.

The first formation of noteworthy size is a large flowstone column against the wall. I call it a column, but it is not truly a column since it does not extend to the floor. Beneath this formation which is very smooth in places, there are mud-colored knobs that have grown from the floor. We continued to descend through the passageway through an area where there was much dead rimstone.

A formation soon loomed before us in the form of two stocky stalagmites that were joined to create a saddle. I was reminded of a large, fancy stock saddle with gala decorations. I snapped a picture of Jack astride the limestone saddle. I began wondering what this formation was dubbed when the cave was operated commercially and the guides sought to give the people their money's worth by pointing out various things locked in the shapes and sizes of the formations. It certainly was no strain on the imagination to see a saddle and even though I am somewhat dubious of slapping a name on a formation to entertain the customers, it was right and proper that this should be a saddle.

The slime mold began to make its appearance in abundance on the decaying wood of the broken down steps and walks. Untrue to its name, at least at this particular stage of its life cycle, the mold had the appearance of carded cotton. It was so delicate and light that even when I touched it there was practically no sensation and it was almost as though I was trying to feel fog. Slime molds are a biological enigma. Within nature there are always exceptions to the rule and slime molds carry this to excess in that biologists are indecisive as to whether they are plants or animals since they display traits of both realms of the living world. Some biologists, out of frustration, have created for the slime molds a little realm of their own between the plant and animal worlds.

Near a large dome over which hung a curtain formation, we descended a rather steep and slippery bank into a large room. To the right, a small passageway lead us through to the room at the end of which is the Stratosphere Balloon formation. Reaching over twice head high, the large formation did indeed appear as a balloon ascending with icicles hanging from its fabric and its gondola encrusted from the iciness of the upper atmosphere. The balloon lies at the end of the cave and has a chamber all of its own. It was an awe-inspiring sight and a calculation of the time that went into the formation of this spectacular flowstone formation is quite staggering. On leaving the cave, I shared exactly the sentiments of Bishop Asbury because all that I had seen had been "awfully grand."

The first road to the left after leaving Stratosphere Balloon Cave and Seneca Caverns will lead one to near the sites of Hellhole and Schoolhouse Caves after driving about two miles. The entrance to Hellhole is located about two hundred yards west of the road through a sink where there is a sheer drop of 180 feet to the floor of the large entrance room. Getting into and getting out of Hellhole Cave requires the use of ropes and a good knowledge of how to use them.

Once the ascent has been made to the floor of the entrance room, two passages lead off with one towards the north that comes to a pit over fifty feet deep which is known as Little Hellhole. The passage east from the entrance room leads into a large room where rock slabs from the ceiling are covered with thick deposits of bat droppings. Shortly beyond this point, the passageway fades out as the ceiling becomes lower and a great deal of "breakdown" has accumulated near here. While Hellhole offers a number of challenges to the spelunker, nearby Schoolhouse Cave is even more challenging.

Fig. 8. The spacious entrance to Schoolhouse Cave does not reveal the difficult and dangerous tasks that face the spelunkers who venture inside. This cave has been heralded as the "toughest cave in America" and has been discussed in several books on caving.

The name of Schoolhouse Cave does not do this cave justice unless one found education torturous. The cave has been the site of at least one death due to a caving accident and recently it became necessary for an experienced and skilled cave rescue team to haul out inexperienced and poorly prepared spelunkers who attempted to explore the cave.

The entrance to Schoolhouse Cave is located in a sink near the road and is large enough to drive a truck through. The cave has been likened to traversing a miniature mountain range with steep slopes and deep gorges in the blackest of night with all of this packed into a distance of 1600 feet which is the length of the cave by the way the bat flies. The various names that have been given certain points in the cave speak of its dangerous features. Such names as Bottomless Pit, Nightmare's Nest, Angel's Roost and Nick of Time reveal the task of exploring the cave which must be undertaken only by experienced and skilled spelunkers who have a good command of mountaineering and rock climbing.

Schoolhouse Cave was the site of saltpeter operations during the Civil War when nitrate deposits were dug in the large entrance room, but it was not until fairly recently that the cave was fully explored and described. Tom Culverwell has reported in the Bulletin of the Potomac Appalachian Trail Club the attempts that were made to fully explore the cave, but attempts that were not realized until 1941. Later that same year, H. F. Stimson and a group undertook the seemingly impossible task of surveying and mapping the cave. Since then the cave has been visited by a number of experienced and skilled spelunkers. Schoolhouse offers a challenge to those persons who are trained and adequately equipped and it is certainly no place for the ill-equipped and the foolhardy.

While a number of the most outstanding caves in the region are located in Germany Valley, no discussion of caves would be complete without a visit to Smokehole Caverns in Grant County west of Petersburg. To the right after entering the caverns, there is a man-made apparatus that has taken its place among the lore and legend of the caverns—a moonshine still, a reconstruction from pieces of stills once operated here before the caverns were commercialized and assumed their present respectable and law-abiding aspects. The still may seem a rather auspicious beginning to a tour of natural wonders, but no one can deny that this contraption has a rightful place in the history of the area and, in remote places in the mountains and hollows, similar devices may continue to condense their liquid lightning.

As one enters the depths of the caverns, he walks along a passageway with the ceiling at times only a few feet overhead. A stream flows along the right side of the corridor until one looks down into a crystal clear pool. Before the caverns were improved for commercialization, entering the caverns had to be along the rocks and other obstacles along the underground stream. There are no formations of any noteworthy size along this passageway and it is not until the ceiling soars to a height of about eighty-five feet that the first large formations are encountered. At this point as I listened patiently while the guide pointed out a prairie dog and an umbrella with his light high on the wall in front of us, I noticed bats being disturbed by the light and fluttering short distances before they came to rest on another formation.

The bats looked small and were probably one of the Myotis species or little brown bats. Most people would look upon these denizens of the dark which look like winged mice as a nuisance or even in horror. I have always held bats in a higher regard than that and have had, for a number of years, a quasi-interest in them. Bats are associated with the unknown, the mysterious and the out of the ordinary and since I have an interest in all aspects of the strange, then I must of necessity have some liking for bats.

For the benefit of those people who think a bat is a bat, there are a half a dozen species found in West Virginia. The big-eared bat is the most bizarre of the bats found in the state with its exceptionally large ears comprising about a third of its body length. The big-eared bat has been found at a number of places in the mountains and seems to prefer caves at an elevation of 2000 feet or more. The big-eared bat has been found in Seneca Caverns and Cave Mountain Cave.

At this point in the caverns where I began to contemplate the status of bats in the scheme of things, the lowest point underground had been reached at 325 feet below the sod. The guide told of a woman who once jokingly said, "Where for such a small price could a person be buried so deep?" Her humor is well taken, but the thought is chilling. In studying the details of the strata overhead, it can easily be seen that the rocks are tilted almost vertically. The caverns and its formations are a great, subterranean crevice and the formations have been created where water seeped through the layers of limestone and came to the surface or along the bedding plane in the parlance of the geologist.

At one point along the corridor, the guide pointed to a mass of rock that had broken loose from the ceiling possibly ages ago and was now held in place by a shelf and the soaring wall. The thoughtful person might calculate the chances of this mass making its final plunge to the floor while he is underground and conclude that the possibilities are infinitely remote. A person is far safer in these natural passageways and rooms which have been sealed and solidified by limestone formations than in a man-made dupe on nature such as a coal mine.

Through a low passage and up a flight of steps lies the wonders of the Room of a Million Stalactites, a fact I was not ready to dispute or had the time to verify, where the caverns abound in wonders and take on magnificent aspects. Two large dome pits in the ceiling are over one hundred feet above the floor. The walk passes a cascading flowstone formation of some length that is called Rainbow Falls. At the crest of the falls, there is a flowstone dome about three feet high from which water bubbles endlessly. The formation has been dubbed, as might be expected, the Fountain of Youth and has been created by the limestone in solution being piled higher and higher.

Almost overhead is one of the most delicately beautiful formations in the caverns and one of the largest. The great Ribbon Stalactite, reputed to be the largest in the world, is about twelve feet in length across the top and sixteen feet in length along its drooping ruffles. Even though the length of time that it takes a formation to grow is quite variable, the age of this spectacular stalactite has been estimated at about four million years. It has the color of tanned skin and its large, delicate ruffles flow downward like an uneven theater curtain. Where the ruffles end, it looks as though some hand at one time had started to push the curtain aside and it had remained forever fixed that way. One would almost expect the curtain to rustle if a gust of wind blew.

Beneath the large ribbon stalactite is a great dome which was being raised as the curtain above was being woven. In an age yet to come, these formations will be one and the curtain will have descended on a drama that took millions of years to act. As one descends the steps to a pool where golden and rainbow trout from the Petersburg hatchery spend the summer, the base of the large dome is reached and it is higher than one's head.

Along the walls above the surface of the water in the pool, limestone coral has been formed and a distinct water mark shows that the level of the water has fluctuated over the ages. A number of formations of various forms and shapes are found in the room beyond the pool. Along with flowstone cascades and various rimstone formations, there is the oddity of a curved stalactite. Since water is supposed to play by the rules of gravity as everything else and in the formation of stalactites fall straight to the floor, this one is a real enigma and how it was able to get to its present length and shape without playing by the rules poses something of a mystery. Along one wall is the Queen's Canopy, a large domed flowstone formation with stalactites hanging from its top.

A short distance beyond the curved stalactite and the Queen's Canopy, the tour of the caverns ends when one comes to a place where a muddy passageway leads upward for about sixty feet to a room. In years to come, this passage may be enlarged, steps built and the room above will become part of the tour and the cave enthusiast will get even more for his money in Smokehole Caverns where he already gets his money's worth in underground wonders wrought in stone.

The greatest flurry of activity that went on in caves before the advent of the spelunker was during the Civil War when clay and silt fills were mined as a source of saltpeter in the manufacture of gunpowder. The economic bind on the Confederacy made the exploitation of caves necessary to obtain saltpeter. Over twenty caves in West Virginia were mined during the way years.

Even though it was during the Civil War that caves received the greatest attention as a source of nitrates, a few operations were underway fifty years before during the War of 1812. Little more than tradition supports the claims that Mill Run Cave and Saltpeter Cave in Pendleton County were mined during the early 19th Century since practically no evidence has been found in either of the caves. In Grant County, at Peacock Cave relics have been found from operations that were supposed to have been carried on by a man named Peacock as early as 1808.

The origin of saltpeter deposits, potassium nitrate and nitro-calcite, has never been fully explained even though a number of theories have been discussed. Bat droppings have been indicated as the source of

Fig. 9. View of the entrance to Trout Cave from within the cave. Exploited as a source of saltpeter during the Civil War, the cave is popular with spelunkers since it offers a number of challenges even though it lacks a variety of formations.

these nitrates, but the small amount of material in bat guano that would form nitrates would seem to discredit this theory. Some caves have large amounts of saltpeter where the conditions are such that it is nearly impossible for large numbers of bats to roost or hibernate. Very little evidence has been found that the saltpeter has been deposited from nitrate material that was present in the limestone before being leached by the circulation of water. In recent years, nitrogen fixation by bacteria has received attention as the answer to the question of how saltpeter deposits originated.

Various relics from the saltpeter operations during the Civil War such as troughs, hoppers and ladders can still be seen in some caves even though these relics have been subject to over a century of deterioration. After the digging of the saltpeter earth, it was placed in wedge-shaped hoppers where water was poured over it in order to leach out the nitrates. The liquid was then evaporated with the saltpeter being left and after some further processing, it was ready for use in gunpowder. A gunpowder mill was in operation near Trout Cave in Pendleton County until 1864 when it was destroyed by a number of Union cavalrymen. Cove Knob, Hoffman School, Schoolhouse and Cave Mountain Caves also show signs of mining operations.

The men and boys who worked the saltpeter diggings were often contemptuously called "peter monkeys" by the soldiers who carried out other duties. Anyone who has been in Trout Cave can easily see how they acquired and even earned their nickname. Most of Trout Cave can be compared to traveling the dry bed of a stream that is strewn with large boulders in the dark. At many places, the floor drops away from beneath one's feet and he can look down into crevices and pits that yawn deep and dark. The main area of digging was located some distance from the entrance and it would have been grueling and torturous work hauling the earth out of the cave. As the men clambered over the rocks, they lived up to their contemptuous nickname. The ceiling of the cave is studded at many places with fossil shells that date from the Devonian sea since the cave is in one of the limestones of the Helderberg series. Standing near the entrance to Trout Cave, one can look down towards the river and see outlined under the sod the remnants of foundations of what may have been the gunpowder mill.

Even though many caves today are the scene of social gatherings where white tie and tails are out of the question and the attitude is rather come as you are as long as you have the proper caving gear, long before the speleological set on the cave scene made their appearance Kenny Simmons' Cave was the sight of many a gala event on the 4th of July at the turn of the century. Located in Pendleton County near U.S. route 220 about five miles from the Virginia line, the relatively level floor of the cave, little more than a large, domed room, served as a dance floor. When people became winded from dancing, a boat ride on the underground lake offered an interesting diversion. The cave provides a natural "tunnel of love" and once a couple rowed onto the lake, only one end of which can be seen from the launching place, any carnival rigged tunnel of love would leave much to be desired by comparison.

As I switched on my head lamp and bent down to go through the low entrance which was dug in 1895, there was no evidence, once inside, that the cave had been the scene of social events. All was still, except for the measured dripping of water and there was only darkness, except where I danced the light along the walls and ceiling. The light revealed a number of formations near the entrance, the most common of which were soda straws along the joints in the ceiling, but also two columns that stood in sharp contrast to one another. One was robust with fringes of flowstone fingers at intervals along its columnar height while the other was slim and slightly crooked--sort of a fire house pole as seen by someone who had had one too many cocktails. Farther on, there was a stalagmite formation that had gone several different directions during the process of formation and ended up looking very much like a cactus.

We walked towards the end of the cave where the ceiling drops to the floor before backtracking to the place where a bank drops sharply to the edge of the small lake. The bank was slippery and the mud at the edge of the water had the consistency of chocolate glue. The remains of a small boat were sunken in the clear water. As I cast the beam of light through the opening, the farthest point I could see without wading into the water seemed about twenty feet away. Actually, the small lake is twenty-five feet in diameter with the ceiling twenty feet above the surface of the water and the water reaching a depth of thirty feet in places.

After clambering back up the bank, we traversed the rocks that had fallen from the ceiling and were banked almost to the ceiling along the east wall. Initials and dates were numerous on many of the rocks and the oldest date I noticed went back more than fifty years. A number of rather large and interesting formations were located in alcoves along the wall. Linton pointed out a freakish sight of a slab of rock that had started to fall, but was now held in place rather precariously by a formation that had grown around it. It appeared almost as a small scaffold secured with ropes with one end sagging dangerously. For him who contemplates such a puzzle, an exact and precise explanation will be about as forthcoming as the case of the curved stalactite.

As we left the cave, with a little imagination, I could almost hear a fiddle whining out the strains of square dance music and I wondered how many young fellows may have met their first love at a social in this cave. Now that would be a real story to tell your children and grandchildren! How times have changed from a day when a cave offered a convenient place for a get-together to today when people enter them with a quasi-scientific determination, but always with an eye for fun. We know our ancestors lived in them, so I suppose there will always be a place in the hearts and spirits of some people for caves.

CHAPTER THREE

THREADS IN A CLOAK OF GREEN

When most of the bite has been taken out of winter and there is the promise of a new season in the air, spring will begin to reveal itself with the thrusting of wild flowers through the brown carpet of leaves on the forest floor and the emergence of leaves to clothe the trees that have stood naked through the winter. Even before the drab hues of winter have been fully replaced by the green of spring, some wild flowers will seem impatient and will thrust their blossoms upward to add color to the drab scene that winter has left in its wake.

During late March and early April, the observant person may find the delicate snow trillium on rocky banks. This little flower seems a good link between the two seasons in that its white petals and leaves that have a frosted look seem more a part of winter than spring, but its small size and delicate nature belong to spring. It makes its appearance when patches of snow may still linger, but it gambles its life that there is enough warmth in the air to sustain it for a few brief days. This little trillium is not a common flower, but it has been found in some numbers in the River Gap near Franklin and near the 4-H camp at Thorn Spring Park.

When the little snow trillium is in bloom, other flowers will be in the process of unfolding their flowers and displaying the colors they will add to the forest floor. While the snow trillium is displaying its delicate white flower, the trailing arbutus will put forth its clusters of small, rosy flowers along its creeping stems with their oval, rough leaves that stay green throughout the year. While the trailing arbutus is found at many places, it seems to have an affinity for evergreens and is found growing quite abundantly beneath the stunted spruce along the Allegheny Front.

The bloodroot will soon be in bloom with its white flower with numerous petals that give it somewhat the appearance of a daisy, but a daisy lacks the red juice that has given this common wild flower its name. The hepaticas, both the roundlobe and the sharplobe, lack true

Fig. 10. A relative of the rhododendron, laurel and azaleas by virtue of it being a member of the Heath family, the trailing arbutus is among the first plants to bloom in the spring when the clusters of rosy flowers make their appearance among the evergreen leaves.

petals, but the sepals are lavender or white and the flower of the hepatica nods in the breeze from the top of a long stem. One of the most attractive of the spring wild flowers is the fawn lily with its yellow bell-like flower that rises above leaves that are mottled with brown. No consideration of spring flowers would be complete without some mention of the spring beauty with its small pink flowers with the deep pink veining and its grass-like leaves. Later in the year one might easily overlook this flower, but during the spring when few flowers are in bloom it is rather outstanding.

These are by no means all of the wild flowers that will be found in bloom during the spring, but these are some of the interesting or showy of spring flowers. As the days of spring pass, the jack-in-the-pulpit, the trilliums, the bellworts, the violets and many other flowers will be in bloom to add color and variety to the season as spring approaches summer.

Before turning to a consideration of other wild flowers or the plants that bloom at various times of the year, let us turn back the pages of the calendar beyond those days in March when the snow trillium was in bloom and even beyond the days of winter to ages ago when a winter prevailed upon the earth that lasted thousands of years. It was during the period of geological history that is called the Pleistocene that the magnificent spruce forests that were originally found west of

Fig. 11. One of the earlier spring wild flowers to make its appearance through the litter on the forest floor is the Dutchman's breeches with its blooms that look like tiny, starched pants that have been hung on a line to toss in the wind.

the Allegheny Front had their beginning. The Pleistocene is the period that encompasses the last million years of the earth's history and is often referred to simply as the Ice Age.

During this long period of time, large ice sheets advanced across the face of the American continent to hold sway with seemingly endless periods of cold weather until they retreated northward and were greatly reduced in size. The expansion and spread of glaciers occurred at least four times and many geologists and climatologists believe that we are living in an inter-glacial period when the climate is warm and the polar ice cap has been greatly reduced. It is expected that one day the great glaciers will again advance southward from the Arctic and much of the earth will again be in the grips of an Ice Age.

During that time when much of the North American continent was greatly influenced by the southward push of the great ice sheet, many northern plants and animals were forced southward as a result of the advancing glaciation and frigid weather. Plants moved southward by dropping their seeds progressively farther to the south in an effort to escape the freezing cold and the crushing weight of the ice. It is reasonable to assume that it was during this time that such coniferous species as spruce and fir were forced southward along with many other northern plants to grow at latitudes far below their home in Canada where they are commonly found today.

As the ice sheet retreated and the climate became warmer, many northern plants were confined to the high mountains where temperature and climatic factors are very similar to the latitudes that the plants normally occupied farther north. We find in the upper Potomac region today relict plants from the vegetation during the time of glaciation. A few plants that are found here were no doubt much more common and widespread during the periods of advanced glaciation. The great ice never covered any of the area that is now the present state of West Virginia and the region doubtless became a refuge for many northern plants and animals.

The paper birch that gave the Indians along the Great Lakes bark to construct canoes is found at a few places in the upper Potomac area such as along the crest of North Fork Mountain and near the old Stony River Dam in Grant County. While the paper birch is found scattered along the high mountains as far south as the Great Smokies, the red pine that is found on North Fork Mountain reaches the southernmost known point of wild or unassisted growth there. This northern pine is also found growing wild on South Branch Mountain in Hardy County where it grows near the outstanding Pocono sandstone cliffs of Helmick Rock.

In ages gone by, both of these trees may have been much more widespread than we find them today, but as the ice retreated and the climate became warmer they disappeared in many places. It was along the high ridges of North Fork Mountain and South Branch Mountain that the paper birch and red pine were to continue to grow high and buffeted by the wind.

It is unfortunate that the early settlers did not leave us a more complete account of the original forests as they found them. It is possible to piece together from the few scraps of information that can be gleaned from various sources a fairly good picture of the original forests of the region before they were changed forever or disappeared before the advances of the lumberman or the destructive and consuming flames of fire.

It seems that much of the area to the west of the Allegheny Front in Grant County and along Spruce Mountain in Pendleton County was cloaked by the dark green of a vast spruce forest. Intermingled with the spruce were such hardwoods as yellow birch, sugar maple, black cherry and beech. Hemlock was also mixed with the towering spruce at various places. The floor of the forest was covered by a thick mat of humus and sphagnum moss grew in a thick carpet at many places beneath the trees. The moss and the spruce worked in a partnership

Fig. 12. The tract of virgin hemlock and northern hardwoods on Saw Mill Run in Pendleton County offers a picture of the original forests that covered the higher elevations of the region. The hemlocks have reached the most impressive sizes with trees measuring nearly four feet in diameter.

for the benefit of the other in that the overshadowing spruce and hardwoods prevented a great loss of moisture from the moss through evaporation. The moss in turn kept the temperature of the earth cool and made it conducive to the growth and spread of the spruce.

The trees in the original forests grew to impressive sizes and the mute remains of hemlocks have been found that were upward to seven feet in diameter. Spruce logs have indicated that the trees were upward to 250 years old when they were cut and the remains of hemlocks have been found that have been given an age of nearly 400 years when they were felled by the axe.

One place that a person can go today in order to gain something of a picture of the original forests of spruce and northern hardwoods that blanketed the high western rim of the region is to the tract of virgin timber on Saw Mill Run about three miles from Cherry Grove in Pendleton County. It is ironic that a piece of virgin forest should survive along a stream called Saw Mill Run, but for many years logging went on all around these trees that were left untouched and a logging railroad was even built along the course of the stream to haul logs from the surrounding mountain slopes.

Most of the trees are hemlocks with the largest ones being about forty inches in diameter at breast height. There is a generous number of red spruce found in the woods with the largest ones falling a few inches short of two feet in diameter. The presence of red spruce seems to point out that this conifer was found at lower elevations originally than it is often found today along the slopes of Spruce Mountain or the Allegheny Front. The hardwoods present include red maple, black birch, red oak, beech and black cherry with the smallest trees having a diameter of eighteen inches.

While this tract of virgin timber is situated on the slopes of a mountain some distance from the area beyond Spruce Mountain and the Allegheny Front, it would still offer a view of the original appearance of the forests at the higher elevations and also some indication of the composition of the primeval forests as to tree species. Even if a person has no interest in trying to construct a picture of the original forests, a visit to the virgin timber is worth-while in order to see the impressive girth and height of many of the trees.

These mighty forests remained intact and practically untouched until about the middle of the 19th Century. At that time the chain of events was set in motion that was to put an end to the original forests along the crest of the Allegheny. Before the middle of the last century, a popular practice to gain pasturage was for farmers to girdle the trees on several acres of land in the limestone country at high elevations. After the passage of a few years, the land was fired in an effort to kill the underbrush and burn fallen timber in order that grass would spring up on which to pasture cattle that would be driven into the area from many miles away.

No doubt the name Dolly Sods has reference to this practice or the clearing of land along the mountain crest to provide grazing for cattle. Cattle are still pastured on the wild expanses of the Huckleberry Plains where they can roam for miles without meeting the confining barrier of a fence. Many acres of pasture are in use in the mountains today that were created originally by killing the trees and setting fire to the resulting litter. At many places, where the underlying rock was sandstone instead of limestone, bracken fern grew up to cover many denuded and nearly worthless acres.

The event that was to have the greatest impact upon the forests along the Allegheny Front was when fire escaped from the camp of Confederate scouts who were camped on the Roaring Plains in Randolph County during 1863. This fire devastated a vast area and was one of many fires that were to rage across the countryside at various intervals almost until the present. These fires were a vital factor in transforming the appearance of many areas to take on many of the aspects they have today.

Fig. 13. View across the Roaring Plains that reveals the rather level nature of the land immediately west of the Allegheny Front where the spruce is wind-swept and a number of northern plants are found. The road to Bear Rocks can be seen in the right of the picture.

The Roaring or Huckleberry Plains just west of the Allegheny Front seem to have been created by a number of fires that have burned across the area during the past century. Some people insist that the area has had its present appearance since the first settlers arrived, but other authorities insist that the present plant life and look of the land has only been in existence a century at most. The Huckleberry Plains have gotten their name from the dense growth of huckleberries and blueberries that are found covering numerous acres along the wind-swept expanses.

Along with the spruce that grows along the Huckleberry Plains in a stunted condition or with the branches all blown to one side, there are a number of shrubs and flowering plants. Besides the huckleberries and blueberries that have been the source of the area's name, there is skunk currant, red raspberry, the black alder which has bright red berries in the fall, the speckled alder, mountain ash, mountain holly and the wild holly that reaches its southern limits in Randolph County. On the ground can be found the painted trillium that blooms abundantly in the spring and the wild bleeding heart that blooms throughout the summer. The dwarf cornel has bright red berries in the fall while the

Fig. 14. The oceanorus blooms abundantly in the bogs on the
Huckleberry Plains during late summer. This lily has a disjunct distribution in that while it is found at high elevations, it also occurs
along the Atlantic Coast.

yellow clintonia has yellow bell flowers in early spring and blue berries in late summer. The fireweed will be found in bloom along the
roadsides during most of the summer. In boggy places, the wood lily,
oceanorus and St. John's-wort can be found in bloom during late summer when the huckleberry pickers appear in numbers to pick the berries that are ripe. Club mosses and ground pines of a few species are
a common ground cover everywhere on the Huckleberry Plains.

When members of the Brooks family of naturalists were at
Spruce Knob undertaking field work during 1908, vast acreages of
land along the mountain had been decimated of the original forests by
fire and the vegetation that had grown up to cover the scarred earth
was bracken and club mosses. While this is the case, there is some
evidence that not far from Spruce Knob, there is a treeless area that
seems to have always been devoid of trees.

Treeless or "bald" areas have been known for sometime in the
Great Smokies where they have been the source of attention and speculation as to what brought about the creation of these "balds" in otherwise heavily forested areas. Various theories have been put forth,
among them the idea that such treeless areas were cleared by the
Indians and used as campsites or places to build signal fires.

It has only been within recent years that "balds" in West Virginia have been the subject of discussion. It seems that Bald Knob in Pocahontas County was devoid of trees when the settlers arrived about 1770 and the treeless nature of the area continues to linger today. The bald areas that are found north of Spruce Knob seem to indicate that a number of factors have been at work and there is evidence that some of these treeless areas have been caused by fire while others show no signs of any vegetation other than grasses. In the areas where there is no evidence of trees having grown originally, Allegheny fly-back grass is the common ground cover.

The lumbering industry brought the final disappearance of the original forests of spruce and northern hardwoods along the western edge of the region. The Western Maryland Railroad was completed along the North Branch of the Potomac in 1887 and a large band mill was built at Dobbin by the Parsons Pulp and Lumber Company and continued to operate for several years. The railroad gave access to nearly the entire northwest corner of Grant County and for a number of years mills were in operation at towns that have now long ceased to exist and have been largely forgotten.

During the early 1900's, the Babcock Lumber and Boom Company of Pittsburgh built large mills at Davis, Tucker County, along the Blackwater River. This company built logging railroads eastward from Davis into the Canaan Valley and along the Stony River and even as far as the Allegheny Front. At this time the Parsons Pulp and Lumber Company was operating mills at Laneville, Tucker County and Horton in Randolph County. These mills drew heavily on the forests of the region and, for sometime, there was a logging camp and railroad switch near the present site of Spruce Knob Lake.

The lumber companies went about cutting the forests of the region until the original forests that had not been scarred by fire were completely gone. In many places even today, as along the Roaring Plains, the land is quite desolate and barren from the logging and fires that followed in the logger's wake a half century or more ago. Fires swept across the land and destroyed the humus down to bedrock making it difficult for revegetation to get underway. The days of logging were exciting and even romantic in the thinking of many people today, but the big mills are gone, many of the log towns are gone and the loggers are either gone or are very old men. The only thing that has remained unchanged is the wind that wails across the Roaring Plains as it has for countless ages.

Again turning to the passage of the seasons and the blooming of wild flowers as spring approaches summer, we will find the white clintonia in bloom with its many small, white flowers set at the top of a stem several inches high above a number of large leaves. The plant

Fig. 15. Named in honor of a Swedish botanist who visited America, the mountain laurel adds beauty to the countryside when it blooms during the early summer and hues of white and pink appear among its evergreen leaves.

is named in honor of DeWitt Clinton who was Governor of New York during the early years of the 19th Century.

The related yellow clintonia is a northern plant that is found at high elevations such as along the Allegheny Front and at Spruce Knob. Unlike the white clintonia that has a number of small, white flowers, the yellow clintonia puts forth a lesser number of pale yellow bell-like flowers during the early spring.

When the white clintonia is in bloom, the mountain laurel will cover many acres with its pink and white blossoms that will make the woods in places seem as though they are piled with snow and many fields become a blanket of laurel in bloom. This evergreen shrub which adds so much color to the countryside when it is in full bloom is known in botanical circles as <u>Kalmia</u> <u>latifolia</u>. It is named in honor of Pehr or Peter Kalm who came to America in 1748 for the Swedish Academy of Sciences in search of plants that could be cultivated in Sweden. The laurel was named in honor of Kalm by his friend, Linnaeus, the describer of many plants collected and sent from America during the colonial period.

As one thinks about some of the plants that have been named in honor of various people, his thoughts may turn to those botanists who have studied the plant life of the region. Many may have been outstanding while others were rather obscure individuals who are little known today, but all of them were dedicated to the forwarding of our knowledge of plants through the collections and studies they made.

The most outstanding early American naturalist to travel through the region of the upper Potomac was Constantine Rafinesque. Many of the details of the life of Rafinesque are beyond our concern at this point, but it is of interest to note that he was born in Turkey in 1783. He came to America and settled in Philadelphia with his younger brother in 1802. At an early age Rafinesque had developed a love for nature and was soon making trips into the countryside to study plants and animals at the expense of his position as a merchant. He returned to Europe in 1805 and lived in Sicily for the next ten years, but the pull of wilderness America was too strong and he returned and set out on a botanical expedition into the Ohio Valley. He served as a professor at Transylvania University in Lexington, Kentucky, for several years before leaving in anger and returning to Philadelphia.

One of the best known incidents in the life of Rafinesque has been recorded by the great bird artist, John James Audubon. Rafinesque visited Audubon while the bird artist was living in Kentucky and the reputation of Rafinesque for being an odd and eccentric person has been furthered by the incident that has been recorded by Audubon in his Ornithological Biography.

Late one night, Audubon was attracted by a commotion in the room where Rafinesque was staying. As Audubon burst into the room, he found his guest running about the room naked swatting at bats with what remained of Audubon's cherished violin. The nude naturalist was soon exhausted and pleaded with Audubon to secure him a few bats because he felt certain they were of a species unknown to science. Out of kindness towards his guest, even though he felt certain they were not a new species, Audubon brought down a few of the bats with what was left of the violin. Audubon makes himself appear as though he has full command of the situation and is able to perform a feat where Rafinesque has utterly failed. Anyone who has tried to strike down a bat knows this is very difficult and it may have been that Audubon was not able to secure specimens as deftly and quickly as he would lead us to believe.

Rafinesque's efforts to find bats that were unknown to science were to be rewarded. On this occasion or on another occasion, he found one of the species of big-eared bats that was new to science and became its describer and reference is often made to this bat as Rafinesque's big-eared bat. In many respects, Rafinesque was to have the proverbial last laugh.

Shortly after his return to Philadelphia about 1825, Rafinesque made a collecting trip up the South Branch River to South Fork Mountain in Pendleton County. It is difficult to determine his exact course, but it may be that he traveled through the Smoke Hole and here we can imagine him hastily examining plants and hurrying about joyfully as he gathered specimens of many plants that were new to him. We can also imagine him as he appears in the village of Franklin seeking lodging for the night. He would have seemed odd to many people as he may have appeared in town towards dusk with his assemblage of equipment such as pressed plants under his arms or in a pack on his back, notebooks sticking from his pockets and his clothes worn from contact with many briars. We can imagine him rushing about the slopes of South Fork Mountain in search of new plants before he began the trip back to Philadelphia.

It is unfortunate that we have practically no record of the plants that were collected in the region by Rafinesque. Most of the specimens he collected during his lifetime have never been found, but fortunately a few have been preserved in the herbarium at the Academy of Sciences in Philadelphia.

Rafinesque died in poverty in 1840 and was buried in Philadelphia. While often being regarded as odd, perhaps his eccentricity was brought about in part by the fact that he was thrilled by all of the new and different things he found in America. There were so many people who could not appreciate Rafinesque's enthusiasm because they did not care, did not cherish and were not concerned about nature as was Rafinesque.

A native of the region who made rather extensive and careful collections of the plant life was Hamilton McSparrin Gamble. Gamble was born in Moorefield in 1838 and at an early age showed an interest in nature and the outdoors. As a youth he made frequent hunting and collecting trips along the South Branch and throughout the surrounding mountains and countryside. He spent some time at the Virginia Military Institute and at the Norfolk Academy before going to Michigan where he began the study of medicine under the supervision of his brother-in-law in 1857. He received a degree in pharmacy from the University of Michigan and was granted his medical degree from Jefferson Medical College of Philadelphia in 1861.

He became a surgeon in the Confederate Army with the outbreak of the Civil War and served in that position throughout the war years. He was imprisoned by Federal forces during the summer of 1863 after he had been placed in charge of the hospitals at Chambersburg following Lee's retreat from Pennsylvania. Following his release, he was attached to a Louisiana regiment before moving to the west where he served under General John Morgan on the raids into Ohio and Indiana. Towards the end of the war, he was attached to the Army of Northern Virginia.

With the end of the war, Dr. Gamble returned to Moorefield to set up his practice of medicine and surgery. He was known widely for his skill as a physician and surgeon and most of the remaining years of his life were spent in Moorefield until his death in 1917. He contributed articles to Gaillard's Medical Journal of New York and was a skilled linguist who spoke several foreign languages. He received an honorary doctorate from West Virginia University in 1894.

During free moments when he was not deeply involved in his medical practice, he botanized in the South Branch Valley. He corresponded with Asa Gray of Harvard and contributed a number of valuable records to the sixth edition of Gray's Manual of Botany. His personal herbarium collection was given to West Virginia University and is one of the oldest portions of the herbarium collection at the university.

Moses Bennett was a good example of a vanishing breed of men. There are still a few old-timers around who possess a knowledge of the value that was placed upon many wild plants for food and medicinal purposes in days gone by. Moses Bennett lived for many years near the summit of Spruce Knob and welcomed a number of distinguished botanists and naturalists into his house which gave him the distinction of living at a higher elevation than any other soul in West Virginia.

Per Axel Rydberg of the New York Botanical Garden visited Bennett in 1925 while collecting at Spruce Knob and gives the mountaineer credit for bringing to his attention the white monkshood that is found at Spruce Knob and at a very few other high points in the state. The party of bird and mammal collectors from the Smithsonian stayed with Bennett during their time of collecting at Spruce Knob during 1936. Bennett gave them a number of valuable notes on the changes that had taken place in the bird life over the years.

Men such as Bennett are a rare breed today and their knowledge of the value of various plants is rapidly being lost. While many people regard much of the medicinal value that was ascribed to certain plants as more superstition than actual fact, the plants that were collected to be used in various potions or concoctions often affected cures in a time when doctors with their knowledge of medicine were miles away or non-existent.

Many men such as Bennett often made a portion of their living as younger men by digging "sang." Many people today have no idea of what is meant when reference is made to "sang" digging or "sangin'." This is a part of our heritage which is rapidly being lost with the past. Ginseng is regarded as having great medicinal value by the people of the Orient. The plant was once widespread in eastern Asia, but nearly

Fig. 16. The most common and widespread of the orchids is the pink lady's slipper that blooms during the spring and early summer in rich woods at all elevations.

disappeared and became very rare as a result of heavy collecting over many centuries. Trade sprang up between the Orient and America where the plant was numerous and for many years "sangin'" was carried on throughout the Appalachians and at many other places in the nation. With the passage of the years, ginseng has grown rare and people no longer dig the plant as they used to and the collecting of "sang" for the China trade is fast becoming a pursuit of the past. Even though this is the case, the value of a pound of dried ginseng roots is around $30 at present and for the persistent and dogged collector there is still some money to be made through "sangin'."

When the calendar marks the summer days of June, the azaleas will be in bloom at numerous places in the woods throughout the upper Potomac region. The rosy honeysuckle-like flowers of these shrubs with their fragrance fill the woods and burst among the green of the spruce along Allegheny Front. The bright orange of the flame azalea seems to set the woods aflame at many places when this shrub is at the height of its blooming.

Due to the wide range in elevations in the region which amounts to thousands of feet, it is possible to find flowers in bloom at the high elevations that have ceased blooming weeks before in the lowlands.

If one missed seeing the attractive pink lady's slipper or moccasin flower in the rich woods at low elevations during the spring, this orchid will be blooming in June under the spruce and at various places at the higher elevations.

During June the nodding red and yellow flowers of the columbine will be common along roads and about rocky banks. Late in the month, the black cohosh will thrust upward its candle-like blossoms and for weeks to come the flowers of this plant will be numerous throughout the woods and along the roadsides.

A showy flower that is to be found at numerous places is the blossom of the prickly pear cactus or "devil's tongue" as it is often called by local people. During the latter part of June and throughout most of July, the prickly pear unfolds its lemon yellow blossoms on the shaly ground along roadsides and in sterile pastures. Along the Rough Run road from Dorcas in Grant County towards Pendleton County, this cactus makes the roadside at many places a carpet of yellow during early July. A similar situation prevails near Fisher in Hardy County where the prickly pear grows abundantly in thick clumps on shaly ground. These are only a few locations of which there are numerous ones where the prickly pear grows and becomes outstanding when it blooms in the summer.

With the blooming of the prickly pear and one's observation of it at many places, it seems fitting to turn to a consideration of a number of rare plants that are found on shaly ground in situations quite similar to those where the prickly pear grows. One of the most interesting and, without a doubt the most unique, aspects of the flora of the region is a number of plants that are restricted to outcroppings of Devonian shale that are found in this part of West Virginia as well as in surrounding counties and in Virginia, Maryland and Pennsylvania at a few locations.

These plants are most often referred to as the "shale barren endemics." The term "shale barren" was first used in reference to the ecological conditions under which these plants were found in 1911 by Edward Steele in a paper describing the appearance of the shale outcroppings and soil on which a number of the endemics were found. He goes on to describe an area near Millboro, Virginia, and states that it is one of the finest areas that he has had the privilege to botanize with its wealth of endemic and rare plants.

While it was not until early in this century that the term "shale barren" came into popular usage among botanists in reference to the endemics found on shaly ground, the history and description of a number of these plants go back much further. Perhaps the first plant that is referred to as one of the shale barren endemics to be collected is the shale or velvet bindweed. This plant was originally collected by the

Fig. 17. Abundant in many places on dry soil, the prickly pear blooms during the middle of the summer when its yellow blossoms make it rather outstanding. The cactus is often found growing in association with a number of rare and endemic plants.

German botanist, Frederick Pursh, near Sweet Springs, Monroe County, in 1805. While on a botanical trip through the Alleghenies, Pursh was attracted to this locality which was gaining a reputation as a spa and here he found, along with a number of other plants, this bindweed which has white flowers that look very much like the morning glory. This bindweed stands erect and forms rather large patches on the shaly soil where it grows. The plant was renamed by Edgar T. Wherry in honor of its discoverer and it now has the Latin name of Convolvulus purshianus.

The best known shale barren in West Virginia is at Kate's Mountain near White Sulphur Springs, Greenbrier County. During the latter part of the last century, Kate's Mountain was to gain wide reputation as the location of the original collection of a number of the shale barren endemics. This seems to have come about by the fact that members of the staff of the New York Botanical Garden often vacationed at White Sulphur Springs. On collecting trips up the slopes of Kate's Mountain they began finding a number of plants that were unknown to science.

For many years, Kate's Mountain was the only known location of the shale barren endemics, but other botanists began to locate sites with geological, ecological and other necessary conditions for the

Fig. 18. Originally believed to occur only on Kate's Mountain in Greenbrier County, the Kate's Mountain clover is now known as one of the most widely distributed of the shale barren endemics.

growth of the endemics some distance from Kate's Mountain. The mountain near White Sulphur Springs was to lose its reputation as the only place on earth where the botanist could see the plants that grew only on the shale.

The yellow buckwheat may be the earliest of the shale barren flora to be collected at White Sulphur Springs on the slopes of Kate's Mountain. This plant was first collected in 1872 by Timothy Allen. This plant prefers the most barren and sterile sites on the shaly soil. Related forms of plants are found in the Rocky Mountains and it has been suggested by Edgar T. Wherry, an authority on the shale barren flora, that the plant ancestor of the yellow buckwheat extended its range across the continent ages ago. Since that time, the plant has been exterminated in many places due to the changing climatic conditions on the continent. Today this endemic buckwheat has a disjunct distribution from related species in the West.

This plant which is a shale barren plant in the truest sense of the term due to its preference for the most rigorous conditions the shale barrens have to offer has been found in the upper Potomac region in Pendleton County south of Franklin.

Not many years after the discovery of the yellow buckwheat, the white-haired leatherflower or clematis was found by Gustav Guttenberg in 1877. The flowers are a dull purple and nod from the end of the branches. This leatherflower has been found along the South Fork River near Brandywine. This area is known for a number of the endemics which is also the case with the area on the Pendleton-Grant line where this leatherflower has been found near the point where route 220 hugs the outcropping shale. In the heart of Grant County, the plant has been found growing near Petersburg.

One of the most famous and widely distributed members of the shale barren flora is the Kate's Mountain clover. This clover was discovered by John K. Small in 1892 on Kate's Mountain. For many years, it was only known from Kate's Mountain where many people came to see it, study it and collect this rare clover. This clover has narrow leaves and a white head that is about the size of the head of a red clover. It is heavy headed and the white blossom often rests upon the ground when the plant is in bloom during April and May. The plant has been found in several counties in Virginia and it is also known from Maryland and Pennsylvania. In the upper Potomac area, there are records for the Kate's Mountain clover from near Upper Tract, near Petersburg and the vicinity of Wardensville.

The shale ragwort or everlasting groundsel was originally collected at White Sulphur Springs in 1897 by Nathaniel Lord Britton and Timothy Allen. This plant has showy woolly white flowers that appear in May and June. It has been found on shale barrens at a number of places in the four neighboring states that lay claim to the unique shale-loving plants.

Another of the endemics that has its type locality at Kate's Mountain is the mountain pimpernel which was collected by Kenneth Mackenzie in 1903. The pimpernel puts forth its yellow flowers in April and May and has been found at several locations on the upper Potomac where the conditions are favorable for its growth.

Other plants which might be considered shale barren endemics are the shale evening primrose and the shale goldenrod. The primrose with its bright yellow flowers seems to have escaped detection as a separate species until early in this century. There continues to be discussion as to whether or not the shale goldenrod is a distinct species. One case in favor of this plant being a separate species and a member of the shale barren flora is the fact that it is the earliest of the goldenrods to bloom and may often be in flower by the end of May.

The shale barren endemics are confined to the exposures of Devonian shale that are found at various places in the region, but there are a number of plants that are able to adjust to the growing conditions on the shaly ground. One of these is the slender knotweed that often grows in abundance on the barrens. The rather obscure mountain whitlow-wort is frequent. The wild pink makes the shale barrens burst with color in the spring when it blooms with its white to deep pink flowers. The bird's-foot violet is an attractive voilet with its floral colors that range from white to lilac to deep purple that likes the shale.

Among the shrubs that can be found growing in close association with the flowering plants on the shale barrens is the dwarf hackberry, the aromatic sumac, the scrub oak and the mountain laurel. The trees are often reduced in size or stunted in their growth, but scrub pine is often common, table mountain pine may be numerous and the chestnut oak is often found growing where the conditions are not too rigorous and forbidding.

Most people who pass the shale barrens even daily have no idea that they support a number of rare and unique plants. Their attention may turn to the roadsides when the prickly pear is in bloom, but throughout the rest of the year the flowers on the shaly ground go unseen. Many of the plants that are endemic to the shale barrens are not showy or especially attractive, but their restricted distribution is what has made them attractive to botanists. The botanist on the shale barren may not find many lovely plants, but he will find a number of plants that are found at very few other places in the world.

One of the richest areas botanically in the region is the Smoke Hole country in Pendleton and Grant Counties. The Smoke Hole canyon extends for some twenty odd miles along the South Branch River from near Upper Tract in Pendleton County to near Cabins in Grant County. The Smoke Hole has long been recognized as a place that offers seclusion and a retreat for the camper and promises a good catch for the fisherman. While many people come to camp and to fish, few of them realize that the Smoke Hole is one of the most botanically rich localities in the upper Potomac highlands, but there is a small group of botanists who are slaves to the lure of the rugged country along the South Branch with its promises of interesting and even rare plants.

A number of factors have been involved in bringing about the rich and varied floral abundance of the Smoke Hole country. This area is located east of the imposing escarpment of Allegheny Front and is not subject to the often severe weather conditions that prevail along the Front and to the west of that mountain ridge. While the Smoke Hole has a lower annual rainfall than does the crest of the high mountains to the west, the growing season is longer in the depths of the Smoke Hole and the average annual temperature is higher than to the west.

These factors have brought about conditions that are favorable to the presence and growth of plants which otherwise might not be found in the area. Here we find that through the extension of their range from along the east coast there are two species of grass, one a lovegrass and the other a bent grass, that have come up the Potomac as far as the Smoke Hole. These are only two examples of how the climatic, geological and ecological factors have favored an abundant variety of plants in the Smoke Hole where the botanist can always find many plants to delight him.

Fig. 19. The rugged Smoke Hole country has long been a haven for the outdoorsman and fisherman. The area offers a wide variety of conditions that influence the presence of a rich and varied plant life which makes the Smoke Hole a botanical treasure chest.

One of the most dramatic and outstanding aspects of the Smoke Hole is the nearly vertical strata of Oriskany sandstone and Helderberg limestone. At numerous places along the rushing course of the South Branch, the cliffs rise high above one's head along both sides of the river. Along the course of the river and at the base of the steep mountain slopes, rich soil has accumulated that offers many trees, shrubs, and flowering plants a good place to send down their roots.

The nearly sheer cliffs are the growing site of a number of ferns that are often restricted to exposures of limestone. Here can be found the black-stem spleenwort with its small evergreen fronds which have a shining black rachis or stem. The rue spleenwort or American wallrue has been found growing on the cliffs and the small fronds of this fern which may grow no higher than two inches lack the symmetry that characterizes the black-stem spleenwort. The purple cliffbrake is often common on the steep rock faces where its bluish-green color is often obscured by the dust that rises from the road during the summer to settle on the surrounding vegetation. The little gray polypody is characterized by its small fronds which are gray in color and scaly in texture. The hairy lip fern may be found on limestone as well as shale and when the weather becomes dry, the fronds will curl and wait for rain before they unfurl.

While a number of ferns are found growing almost exclusively on the limestone cliffs, there is a large number that are not as specialized in the growing conditions that they need and will be found at many places in the rich soil in shady places. One of the most attractive and delicately beautiful of the ferns is the maidenhair fern.

As one begins the drive into the Smoke Hole, the rhododendron will be in bloom during late June and early July along the road where it skirts the side of the mountain some distance above the river a mile or so from the bridge near Upper Tract. At several places near this point, the rhododendron grows with its large, evergreen leaves that set it apart from the laurel with its much smaller leaves. The blossoms of the rhododendron are also much larger than those of the laurel. The rhododendron is found at various locations where there are the conditions such as dampness that it needs, but it is much less common in the upper Potomac region than it is to the west where there is a greater amount of annual precipitation. Along the upper Potomac conditions are more favorable for the growth of the mountain laurel which grows under drier conditions and is found abundantly throughout the region.

The accumulated soil in the ravines and at the base of the steep slopes in the Smoke Hole supports the growth of a variety of forest trees and here such trees as the sugar maple and yellow poplar often grow to impressive sizes and heights. Other trees that are found along the lower slopes of the mountains are the mountain magnolia, butternut, black oak and white ash. Such smaller trees as the pawpaw, redbud and dogwood are often common. The climbing Dutchman's pipe is often found at many places in the woods where it can be recognized by its large, heart-shaped leaves.

The higher and more exposed mountain slopes where the soil is often shallow is characterized by an abundance of chestnut oak with other oaks such as the red oak, black oak and white oak being present. Scrub oak and laurel are found in the understory and chestnut sprouts are often common. The largest chestnut oak in the Smoke Hole is a massive tree that is forty-five inches in diameter which grows by the road a short distance from where one begins the drive towards the fire tower on North Fork Mountain after leaving the river.

The twinleaf with its two-parted leaf that has the appearance of large mouse ears can be found along the path towards Cave Mountain. The twinleaf has a white flower that appears in May, but this plant is most easily recognized by its divided leaf. The blue cohosh grows near where the twinleaf is found and this cohosh has blue berries in the fall.

The rather small, but beautiful showy orchis can be found in bloom during May and June. This orchid has several flowers that are about an inch long with the lip of the flowers being a white or purplish in color. The petals are a lovely shade of purple and are grouped to

Fig. 20. One of the showiest of late summer wild flowers is the cardinal flower which grows near streams and puts forth its bright red flowers that often seem to flame amid the surrounding vegetation.

form a hood. The showy orchis is found in rich soil where it can be recognized when it is not in bloom by its rather large, oval leaves.

During July, the scarlet wild bergamot will be in bloom at damp places near the river where its bright colors will attract the hummingbird to come and sip nectar from the flowers. About this time, the jewelweed or touch-me-not will begin to bloom with its small orange, cup-like flowers that attract hummingbirds to where it grows in moist woods or close to water. The juice of the jewelweed is a good treatment for poisoning from poison ivy and I have noted that these two plants are often found growing in close conjunction.

One of the most outstanding and conspicuous flowers to be found along the South Branch during the latter days of summer is the cardinal flower. I have found it growing on gravel islands in the river near the recreation area in the Smoke Hole and at a few places hugging the bank of the river where its bright red flowers were outstanding among the surrounding greenery. The cardinal flower has a stalk and leaves that are unattractive and give the plant a rather weedy appearance, but the bright red flowers that top the stalk make up for the lack of attractiveness in the stem and leaves.

When the cardinal flower is in bloom, one should look for the great blue lobelia which is related to the preceding species, but which has blue flowers in a lesser number than does the cardinal flower with its red flowers. The blue lobelia is most often found in damp soil near streams. This flower is one of the latest of the more attractive flowers to remain in bloom as summer draws to a close and it can be found in bloom well into September.

While it is not one of the most beautiful plants to be found in the Smoke Hole, the crested coralroot is no doubt the rarest to grow there. The crested coralroot lacks leaves, but it has scales on its bronzy-colored stalk which may grow to a height of two feet. The few flowers are bronze with purple stripes and the lip of the flower has six purple-tipped ridges which has reference to its generic name of Hexalectris. The crested coralroot reaches the northern limits of its range in the Smoke Hole where it is found on the steep slopes growing in numbers at one location, the only known spot in West Virginia..

One cannot fully appreciate the steepness of many of the slopes in the Smoke Hole until he has climbed some of them in search of plants or simply as an acceptance of the challenge they offer. At many places, it becomes necessary to pull oneself upward with the secure branches of trees and shrubs. The climb up the slope must often be made with labored and calculated steps in order to keep from sliding backwards in the loose rock. Descending the slope will be much easier and less tiring than climbing up, but one must be careful and move cautiously downward often making his way from tree to tree to slow his descent. At many places, the slopes are so steep that a person lacks little in being able to look directly down at the road or into the river.

The crested coralroot has found a safe and secure location at which to establish the northern limits of its range where it grows on steep slopes that are often extremely difficult to climb. Indeed one of the floral treasures of the Smoke Hole for the conscientious botanist is the crested coralroot, but one will have to work hard to find it.

The silvery whitlow-wort that grows on the Tuscarora sandstone can be found in the Smoke Hole where this sandstone outcrops and it is also found not far away along the crests of North Fork Mountain and New Creek Mountain. Another name for this plant is nailwort. The common names of this plant come from a reference to an inflammation around the finger or toe nails. It was formerly believed that this plant had medicinal value in curing such an inflammation. The plant is found growing only on the Tuscarora sandstone where the sandstone has been weathered to create soil sufficient for growth. It is found at a number of places on the Tuscarora sandstone, but one of the easiest places to reach where it grows is at the top of Seneca Rocks.

In the Potomac highlands, it almost seems that the plant life from the four points of the compass has come together here to make the region a delight for even the most sophisticated botanist. Down from the North ages ago came such plants as the paper birch and red pine to grow quite alone and at the mercy of the winds on the high ridges. Certainly the most outstanding aspect of the northern plants are those that are found along the Allegheny Front and Spruce Mountain where the land has a look that is very Canadian. From the East, came, among others, the oceanorus that was able to make the leap from the Atlantic shore to the bogs in the mountains. During the summer, when the prickly pear is in bloom over a large area a person might easily think that he was on a rocky slope in the deserts of the West. Many plants that might be thought of as southern such as the orchids that are abundant in the tropics have found their way north to plant such treasures as the crested coralroot and the showy orchis. While plants from the points of the compass have enriched the flora of the region, there are the unique aspects of the plant life that are found at only a few other places in the world such as the endemics on the shale and the silvery whitlow-wort on the sandstone. There are many threads in the cloak of green at the headwaters of the Potomac and the one who pursues plants will find many discoveries to reward his time and efforts.

CHAPTER FOUR

WINGS OVER THE MOUNTAINS

A bird brings different responses to different people. On the part of many people there may be no response of appreciation at all-- the bird goes unseen and unheard. On the part of another person, there may only be a thrill at its colors without any thought or concern about what species it may be. A person with an interest in bird study may see a bird familiar to him or if he has not seen it before, he may seek its name and description in a bird guide. For a person with an interest in history, the sight of a bird today may turn his thoughts to what birds were once found in his region, but have since vanished or been exterminated completely. His thoughts may turn to days now gone in an effort to construct a mental picture of the sights and sounds that once were, but will now remain unseen forever.

There can be no doubt that the passenger pigeon once winged its way over the ridges and valleys of the upper Potomac in sky darkening flocks that flew with a deafening roar. Let no one doubt the power of man to destroy utterly and completely. The passenger pigeon stands as a classic example that when human forces are turned against a species mercilessly and unremittingly it can be destroyed completely. The passenger pigeon was probably the most numerous bird ever to exist on the face of the American continent. During the last half of the 19th Century, the slaughter went on with gun, trap, club, net and all matter of devices for killing until, by 1900, the bird was no longer worthy of profitable pursuit. The last known bird died in the Cincinnati Zoo in 1914.

The Pigeon Roost fire tower on Allegheny Front Mountain not far from Bismarck got its name from the surrounding forests having been a roost for the passenger pigeon until the bird disappeared from the area when the species faced extinction. The stories that have persisted about this roost are much the same as those told about other roosts. The trees were often broken by the weight of the thousands of birds pouring into the roost at dusk. The pigeons were often killed for food during the

fall and early winter. They were said to have been present throughout most of the year and could strip a wheat or buckwheat field of
every grain within a few hours. The birds were such voracious grain
eaters that as a man was trying to scare them from one end of his
field, others would fly in to feed at the opposite end.

The way in which the accounts of this roost differ from other
stories told about the passenger pigeon is in the circumstances con-
cerning their disappearance. Supposedly, the last time pigeons were
seen at the roost was late in the 1880's when flocks were leaving the
roost and flying west in an exodus that lasted three days and at times
darkened the sky. The belief lingers in the area that this was a godsend
and the bird that was such a nuisance was sent into oblivion by an act of
the Almighty. Though many fanciful stories are told about the reasons
for the disappearance of the pigeon, the simple fact remains that it was
relentless slaughter that put an end to the species.

Never again will the sight of a flock of passenger pigeons num-
bering possibly in the millions darken the sky over any part of the
American countryside. Records and accounts written by witnesses of
such flocks and the mayhem of the roosts and nesting sites read like
the fabulous tales from an imaginative mind. Though a person today
may read such accounts with unbelief, there is no doubt that they are
indeed true. This is a fact we cannot erase by our feeling of guilt for
our ancestor's thoughtlessness and we may stand in their defense with
the conclusion there were not as many pigeons as they thought or else
they would have been unable to shoot them down almost to the last
bird. The inescapable fact remains, there were that many birds and
men did blast the species into the black void of extinction from which
there is no return.

Today the turkey finds refuge on the slopes of the higher mountains. The turkey seems to have been fairly abundant when the settlers
first came on the scene. References are made in various early journals
to the abundance of turkeys around clearings in the primeval forests.
The turkey may have even benefited by the clearing of the forests in
those early days. As the original forests vanished and hunting pressure
became heavy, the bird began its decline in numbers and was forced
to seek haven as far as possible from man on the high ridges. Constant
hunting with firearms over the years has made the turkey one of the
most difficult of game birds to bag due to it having become very wary.
Originally it seems to have been a rather tame bird and fairly easy to
bring down, but there has been a complete transformation of the nature
of the wild turkey.

When it is time for courting and nesting to begin, the turkey
cock will gobble usually just after sunrise in order to attract females
to him. He will drive away other males and mate with as many hens as

Fig. 21. The wild turkey was common when the first settlers arrived, but hunting over the years and the encroachment of civilization has caused their numbers to decline until they are now restricted to the higher elevations. Photo of a drawing by the late Tressie Boggs Rexrode of Fort Seybert.

he can attract. The hen lays eleven or so eggs in a slight depression lined with a few leaves. The chicks develop rapidly and are able to fly well enough when they are a month old to start roosting with the adult birds in thick stands of evergreens. As the young bird grows to maturity, the tail feathers will develop brown tips which is a mark distinguishing the wild turkey from the domestic bird with white-tipped tail feathers.

A flock may range over a few square miles from the roost during the day in search of food. There is very little a turkey will pass up in its search for food. Delicious looking tree fruit, flower heads, grass stems, leaves and insects will all be eaten and they will scratch for roots. The chestnut blight took a big item out of the turkey's menu and now acorns have become a staple food. Turkeys benefit greatly from the grain planted for wildlife in forest clearings by the Department of Natural Resources.

A bird receiving much attention in recent decades due to its appearance in places where it supposedly does not belong is the golden eagle. Maurice Broun, curator of Hawk Mountain sanctuary in Pennsylvania, was the brunt of much incredulity when he began to report golden eagles shortly after the refuge land was wrestled from the hawk shooters during the 1930's. Some people insisted the golden eagle was a bird of the western plains and mountains and was not found in the East.

Some of these hard to convince persons made the trek to Hawk Mountain only to have their bold proclamations shattered when Broun showed them golden eagles soaring south over the mountain. Often more than one eagle has been seen in a day leaving little doubt in the mind of the most doubtful person that the golden eagle does indeed appear regularly in the East in migration. In his book, Hawks Aloft, Broun speculates as to where these birds originate and ventures a guess of the area around Hudson Bay in Canada.

When the interested person delves into the writings on the habits of this eagle, he finds fragmentary evidence that the golden eagle once nested in the East and may possibly continue to hold out in the fastness of remote parts of the Appalachians. The upper Potomac highlands seem to be a place where the golden eagle was found until fairly recently and may have nested even though no nest was ever found. In his book, The Appalachians, Maurice Brooks writes that there was once a good population of golden eagles in the mountains at the Potomac headwaters. He tells of seeing seven of the big birds at one time over North Fork Mountain riding the air currents. For anyone who may ask the question as to what has happened to them during the intervening years, Brooks answers it by commenting on the number of mounted birds that can be seen in stores, post offices, filling stations and other places. The intense campaign of varmint control and bounty killing during the 1930's and 40's eliminated the eagles found in the region throughout the year.

Even though it is doubtful that the golden eagle is found throughout the year in the region, it still turns up in the field of view of birdwatchers who perch on the rocky outcroppings and fire tower catwalks during the fall to watch the migration of hawks. The bird has been seen from Bear Rocks on Allegheny Front Mountain and I saw my first pair of golden eagles over Peters Mountain in Monroe County during September of 1957. The bird enthusiast who examines closely all big birds, especially during the fall, may eventually meet the object of his search and know the thrill others have known when they saw their first golden eagle.

The person who keeps the vigil with the hawk-watchers may see his first golden eagle, but even if he does not, he may see more birds

Fig. 22. Even though the golden eagles that were once found at the Potomac headwaters throughout the year seem to have been eliminated, this spectacular bird continues to be seen by the hawk-watchers who find vantage points along the high ridges from which to watch the migration of birds of prey.

of prey in one day than he has seen during his lifetime. Hawk-watching has gained much popularity among bird students in recent years and every year during the sunny days of September more of them hunt out vantage points along the ridges from which to watch the passage of the hawks into the southern horizon.

A successful day depends upon a number of factors, but particularly upon favorable weather conditions. This varies with locations, but it seems that a steady wind striking the mountain and being deflected upward is an absolute necessity for most places. The hawks ride the rising air currents with little more effort than an occasional flap of their wings to correct their course. A variety of weather conditions may develop into a day when a thousand or more hawks may be seen. Such a day may be sparked by foul weather over a period of time only to have a flood of hawks released when the weather clears. The hawk-watcher who is on the ridge when the weather has cleared after a period of bad weather may be in for the thrill of his birding days.

The broad-winged hawk is a species possessing a highly developed habit of migration. During September, particularly during the latter part of the month, the broad-wing is on the move in flocks that may number several hundred birds. The broad-wing is not the only bird to be seen as other hawks in lesser numbers are also drifting south.

Bear Rocks on Allegheny Front has become a popular place from which to watch hawks and often thousands have been seen from this point in a day. The last time I was there on a Saturday in mid-September, the weather was not favorable for large numbers of hawks to be on the move, but still a number of birds were observed. Several times during the morning, flocks of thirty or so broad-wings came circling up out of the valley from beyond our vantage point, rising higher and higher, moving among themselves making a count difficult, until they began to peel off and drift down the ridge.

A marsh hawk on the hunt came coursing low over the stunted spruce with its white rump patch flashing. A sparrow hawk shot by, a Cooper's hawk passed over alternately flapping and soaring and a red-tailed hawk circled overhead with its rufous tail visible when it banked in its circling. Three ravens put on a superb show as they came flying up the ridge calling their harsh croaks while diving at one another, somersaulting and gliding with their black forms set against the blue sky clearly defining their heavy bills and wedge tails.

In the spruce forests that cap the Allegheny Front as well as many of the high ridges to the west, the little saw-whet owl seems to be found throughout the year. Smaller than the widespread and common screech owl which it resembles somewhat in appearance although lacking the ear tufts, the saw-whet owl goes unnoticed by many persons unaware that it even exists and by birders who would like to make its acquaintance. It is a secretive little owl and quiet throughout most of the year except during the early spring when it calls its whistled notes that have been fancied to resemble the filing of a saw.

During October of 1959, Dr. George Hall and Gordon Knight from West Virginia University were manning their mist nets at the Red Creek camp grounds near Bear Rocks when much to their suprise and delight they found a saw-whet owl while checking the nets after dark for entangled bats which can play havoc with a net. That was the first of these little owls netted by Dr. Hall and others who have manned this place in the years since. Another saw-whet owl was caught the same fall and several have been netted and banded in subsequent years. Six of the little owls were plucked from the nets during the fall of 1965.

Reddish Knob, in the southeastern corner of Pendleton County atop the backbone of Shenandoah Mountain that separates West Virginia from Virginia, has been a place where hawk-watchers have gathered on

Fig. 23. Hawk-watchers at Bear Rocks on Allegheny Front Mountain which has gained popularity within recent years as a good point from which to watch the migration of hawks where thousands of the birds have been seen in a day.

a number of occasions within recent years to take up their vigil. The fire tower on the knob offers a commanding view in all directions and this is of particular advantage to the hawk-watcher so that he can keep tabs on the direction of flight of the birds along the mountain slopes since it may change with a change in the movement of the wind and air currents. While the vast amount of country that is open to view helps the careful watcher keep many hawks from slipping by uncounted, it also unfolds some of the most beautiful vistas in the Appalachians.

At Reddish Knob, a person is often alone with the wind, the view and his thoughts. The furrowed buttresses of the mountain drop towards the Valley of Virginia. Early in the morning, when the valley is not hidden beneath haze, flecks of silver in the morning sun betray buildings, houses and rooftops in the wide expanse of the floor of the valley. The Massanutten comes to an abrupt end beyond Harrisonburg and beyond is the Blue Ridge. To look down the slope of the mountain and across the historic Valley of Virginia which has known the footsteps of the first thrusts into the westward mountains and the tread of armies clad in blue and gray is a stirring sight. While the valley has rich and varied memories from its past, from Reddish Knob the events that have given the valley its fame and romance seem far away in time and space. The valley looks gracious and prosperous as it should, but on the mountain one is far away from the hustle in the towns that will mark a new day and there is only the calling of birds and the rush of the wind.

Along the western side of Shenandoah Mountain, the radio tele-scope near Sugar Grove is cocked like a great ear listening to the mur-muring of the heavens while, nearby, a great patch of brown marks the site where the monstrous scope was started, but never rose beyond part of the foundation. The houses of Sugar Grove are snug at the foot of the mountain and seem much more in keeping with the mood of the country than the radio telescope that rises in sharp opposition to the little com-munity. From Reddish Knob, it seems that all of Pendleton County is visible to the northwest on a clear day and it may even be possible to see a few points beyond the bounds of the county. It is often difficult to be certain just how far one can see because many mountains and valleys rise and fall to the west and it is easy to become lost and confused in visual travels to the horizon.

On a morning late in September, a stiff, biting wind was blowing out of the west shearing the mountaintop. The most hospitable spot, the best place to escape the force of the wind, was along the catwalk on the east side of the fire tower. This was not only the place that offered the best refuge from the wind's blast, but was the best vantage point for seeing any hawks which might attempt a ride on the sweeping currents of air and appear out of the north. As time passed, it seemed the last two times that I had come to Reddish Knob had offered the extremes of weather conditions for hawk flights with both being unfavorable. On a previous occasion, there had been no wind and now it seemed there was too much. Even though this seemed to be the case, more hawks were observed than previously and under much more spectacular conditions.

The wind was striking the mountain and then was shot upward. On several occasions, hawks suddenly came up from along the east side of the mountain to hang suspended on the rising air currents before sailing out over the valley or towards the south after making a long curve out over the west side of the ridge. On the previous occasion when there had been practically no wind, the hawks had drifted up lazily seeking a favorable current and often to no avail before they settled back into the trees to wait for another chance or another day. This was not the case on this date when it seemed that as soon as a hawk released its grasp on a limb an updraft rushed it skyward.

Numbers of broad-wings were still around and as we watched from the tower scanning the sky with our glasses would appear seem-ingly from nowhere over the ridge to the north and drifting to the west on bent wings with tails tightly clenched. Most of the birds, after flying towards the west for some distance, would make a rather wide circle towards the south before rocketing out of sight. Many of the broad-wings were seen traveling alone, but on a few occasions groups of a half a dozen of these hawks with the wide bands on its tail were seen as they winged their way southward.

Even though many of the hawks were difficult to identify because their bodies and wings were tensed as they swam through the ocean of moving air, others offered us excellent opportunities to study them closely as they hovered over the ridge near the tower. Most of the hawks that were seen during the day were red-tails and this was the species that seemed to gain the greatest enjoyment out of hanging suspended in the air. One red-tail had checked the tension between the air and its wings so correctly that the greatest movement of its body was its head as it looked first this way and that at the ground. The alula or false wing could clearly be seen on the bird's wing and it is believed that the alula breaks the flow across the surface of the wing and limits the lifting power. The dark breast, clear belly and the pale underside of the tail could clearly be seen as the bird was fixed almost overhead. After making certain there was no mouse or prey of any kind on the ground, the hawk plummeted into the trees along the east side of the ridge crest. On one occasion, a red-shouldered hawk came by close enough for us to see the fine, light bands on the dark tail and the rusty shoulders.

Even though other birds may have failed us, we could depend on the ravens of Reddish Knob to keep things from being dull and to put on a performance when things started to slow. We had no sooner arrived than the ravens cruised by and croaked just to let us know they were not their lesser black brethren the crow. In order to add a little spice to their aerial gymnastics, they began playing tag with a red-tail and, even though it looked as though they started something which could become serious business, it all seemed to have been in fun when they called a halt and the red-tail moved on. We got a very close look at the ravens as we were leaving the mountain when the pair were perched near the top of a large, dead tree with their heavy bills and shaggy throats visible without binoculars before they saw us and flew away silently.

The height of the migration of hawks over the mountain ridges is during the latter days of September when the broad-wing often moves south in flocks that number in the hundreds, but this is certainly not the only reward for the vigilant hawk-watcher as migration lingers on into the fall with red-tails, red-shoulders and other species. Only during September can one see the large flights of broad-wings and only during the fall can one watch the migration of hawks since there is no similar migration in numbers or in magnitude in the spring. Once a person has taken his place among the hawk-watchers along the mountain ridges and has watched the beauty in form and flight as the hawks ride the air currents into the southern horizon, when the calendar again marks the sunny days of September the high and lofty places will beckon where the hawks respond to the annual impulse that has lasted for countless ages.

During the month of October, the trees are aflame with the colors that began to kindle in September and will fade, wither and fall in November. On a Saturday in mid-October, my family and I drove to the top of Spruce Knob. The weather was temperamental with alternate clearing and overcast as we drove up the slopes of the highest mountain in West Virginia. The display of fall colors was indescribably beautiful all along the way and it seemed as though around every bend in the road a new array of autumnal hues burst into view. We had by chance made our trip at precisely the right time, at precisely that moment when the chemical processes within the leaves had completed their work with crowning glory and maximum beauty.

The sky was a somber and threatening gray when we reached the top where it was cold and a strong wind was blowing. As we walked from the car to the pile of rocks marking the highest ground in the state, a red-tailed hawk sailed overhead on bended wings. A sparrow hawk soon shot by trying to correct its course against the strong wind. Hawks were still on the move even though the flood of their migration had passed. Both of these birds were set on gaining distance and a warmer climate in order to escape winter's blasts which, at that moment, must have seemed close on their heels.

The juncos were singing a rather muted and abbreviated song in the stunted spruce, their last fading notes before the howling winds of winter silenced them completely. Down over the mountainside, a raven was calling its harsh croaks. The whole scene spoke of the nearness of winter. Even though winter did not officially begin for another two months, winter comes early to these lofty heights. To the birds and animals at this high elevation the calendar meant nothing, but the bite of the wind meant it was time to move south, seek lower elevations or find a comfortable place to sleep for the coming months.

Winter cold and few birds can dull the enthusiasm of the birder, but curiosity will gnaw until he makes his foray afield to see what birds are still around as well as what northern species may be spending the winter in his locality. Curiosity as well as the responsibility of conducting one of the many Christmas bird counts for the National Audubon Society called me into the open on a Wednesday late in December. The weather during the early part of the week following Christmas had been clear and mild. In order to take advantage of the fair weather, I decided it was time to act. I did not want to be caught by bad weather which could not only dampen the day and my enthusiasm, but also keep down the number of birds on the list.

I started the day at 5 a.m. about two hours before daylight in an effort to hear some owls. Along the river above Upper Tract and from the top of South Fork Mountain to the ridges along Dry Run above Franklin, I tried most every place where I thought there was any chance of success without hearing one. There was light in the east and I was ready to call a halt to owl hunting when I heard the great horned. I was on Thorn Creek above Franklin where the mountains rise sharply from the creek. I sprang from the car and listened intently when I thought I heard the hooting of the big owl. Was it only my imagination creating what I wanted to hear? Several times the bass hoot sequence came from the hardwoods and pines above the sheer cliffs on the mountain face. This big, hardy bird was becoming vociferous as its mating time was near while lesser birds were cowering from the cold seeking only to survive.

After hearing the owl, I drove to Franklin to meet Carolyn Ruddle and John Dorsey who wanted to help me with the count. Our first stop was one of the feeders in town where we picked up a few species which included several cardinals, a white-breasted nuthatch calling its nasal notes and a small flock of goldfinches that flew overhead.

From Franklin, it was back to Thorn Creek to try around the 4-H camp for some of the more common birds we had not gotten. The blue jays and black-capped chickadees were found in the hemlocks. I stepped on a brush heap by the creek rustling it and a song sparrow sprang out and flew across the creek. The bird seemed to show consternation as it looked back to see what had shaken it from its lair. The laughing and hammering of a pileated woodpecker came from on the mountain side.

The real thrill of the day occurred as we were walking up Dry Run on the lower slopes of the mountain through an area of white pines and hemlocks. Some chickadees and a nuthatch were working in the hemlocks and we were watching them and listening in an effort to pick up other species. A couple of times nearby I heard a strange sound, but could not pinpoint its location. A flock of about twenty-five birds soon flew overhead and landed in a hemlock. Even before I put the binoculars on them, I was thinking "crossbills." As soon as I saw the white wing-bar on one of them, I knew they were white-winged crossbills.

Crossbills seem to me to be among the most active and quick birds I have ever seen. They appear very nervous and high-strung, but they are supposed to be rather tame and we were able to move very close to them without them seeming to be bothered by our presence. When one starts to move, they all move. When they fly, they make a rather loud, static chip as the flock flies fast and compactly, often turning sharply and wheeling around several times before landing in a hemlock or pine. The flocking instinct seems to function even while they are feeding because when one moves up or down in a tree or into a nearby tree, the others move accordingly.

This was a new bird for me. I had made the acquaintance of its close relative, the red crossbill, on Gaudineer Knob on Shaver's Mountain in Pocahontas County a few years ago. Now I can say that I think the white-wing is the more attractive of the two crossbills. It was a beautiful sight as these rosy red finches moved about against the green of the hemlocks. This was the 13th bird on the list for the day--lucky 13! Later in the day, we saw a flock of about the same size near Deer Run.

After the crossbills had flown out of sight to search for other cone laden evergreens from which to extract the seeds, we drove to the Dahmer farm near the top of the mountain where they feed the birds. Here we made a few additions to the list with the most important ones being a flock of thirty-two pine siskins and a half a dozen ruffed grouse I flushed from a white pine thicket. The siskins call a chipping note, but they also have a long, buzzing note they all seem to emit together which becomes rather loud and is a characteristic sound for a flock of siskins. The only other bird we needed to top the day off as a northern finch day was the evening grosbeak, but we failed to find them even though some people had reported them at their feeders during the last few days.

The evening grosbeak is a bird that has attracted much attention within recent years due to its extension of its range and particularly for its invasion of much of the nation during recent winters. A century ago, the bird was unknown in the East and was considered a bird of the Northwest. About the turn of the century, it began making its appearance during the winter in New England and, since that time, has gradually extended its breeding range as well as its wintering grounds. Two decades ago, the bird was almost unknown in West Virginia, but now they appear in large numbers during the winter with a regularity of every two years. For the past decade, this pattern has not failed and a winter with few if any grosbeaks present has separated years when they were around in large numbers.

When we reached the foot of the mountain, we stopped along the river to see if we could find anything new to the list. Out of sight down the river came the rattle of a belted kingfisher, but the bird did not seem to want to come our way and be seen. The thought came to Carolyn and me about the same time to try at the low water bridge at Franklin where the kingfisher is often present fishing. We had no sooner gotten there than a kingfisher flew into sight, landed and began scolding with its rattling voice before it flew on. This may have been the very same bird we had heard a few minutes before and we had made it to the bridge with only seconds to spare.

Throughout the rest of the day, new additions to the list became increasingly difficult to find. We crossed a couple of mountains during

Fig. 24. While the mourning dove is a summer resident when it will be heard calling its mournful coos, it also spends the winter in numbers when flocks will be found roosting in thickets of evergreens or gleaning food from the fields.

the day, but the only bird that was up there was a red-tailed hawk. We had pulled up at the Deer Run Methodist Church when a large bird was seen circling just over the trees along the ridge. It wheeled around just enough times for us to catch the rufous tail before it dipped out of sight. Near the mountain tops, there was not the sound of a bird, only the wind moaning through the pines. We drove on and dropped down off of the mountain into Fort Seybert.

At the Dyer farm where the birds are served a winter board, we found numerous individuals of species we had tallied during the day except for the Carolina wrens. We found four of the reddish sprites around the buildings and in the bushes before we left. Several cardinals were about along with downy woodpeckers, mockingbirds, chickadees, titmice and a few red-bellied woodpeckers.

A flock of over a hundred mourning doves was flushed from a field of corn stubble where they were feeding. Our attention had been attracted to them by a few perched on a fence by the field. We began walking towards them when others flew up fanning their tails to show the white and with their wings whistling.

Even though there was still an hour or so of daylight left, the day as far as birds was concerned was over. We reviewed the list and found we had twenty-seven species with six hundred individual birds.

Our curiosity satisfied and my responsibility fulfilled, we called it a day. I was content for the present, but I knew the gnawing would begin anew until I could only overcome it by the formula of the open air, woods and fields and looking through binoculars to see what birds are around. Such is the fate of the birder and once the thrill of the count and the sight of birds has gotten into his blood, he is a slave to their songs, their beauty in flight and their flashing colors forevermore.

When the inhospitable weather of winter keeps one indoors, it gives a person opportunity to reflect upon the past year recounting experiences or to anticipate the coming of spring and new discoveries. The person with an interest in birds may spend time typing field notes hastily jotted down weeks or months before while recalling those observations that now spring vividly to mind. The long evenings of winter provide a good opportunity for assessing bird numbers and distribution from such notes and also time for the planning of trips into untramped locations that may yield something new and interesting.

The Potomac highlands offer a variety of bird life to satisfy the ornithological appetite of anyone from the amateur bird student to even the most conscientious and experienced birder. The topography of the region, the valleys and ridges, has created conditions to the liking of many northern and southern species. Birds usually considered characteristic of more northerly latitudes find conditions along the high ridges very much to their needs and stay to nest. The long, unbroken valleys offer avenues for the northward wanderings of birds most often thought of as southern. Here northern birds meet southern birds, overflowing one another to nest only a few thousand feet apart to make the whole region a delight for the ornithologist.

Birds characteristic of the North make their summer home along the high ridge of the Allegheny Front. The spruce forests yeild a number of birds one would normally find quite common in similar places in Canada. The little golden-crowned kinglet is found in the spruce and is more often heard singing its wiry notes than seen. The virtuosos of the bird world, the thrushes such as the Swainson's thrush and the veery, are also found during the summer when they can be heard singing their ethereal songs that blend into a chorus shortly before dark. The magnolia warbler with its bright yellow breast is like a flame in the spruce as it flies from place to place singing its clear notes.

Other birds common in northern areas should not be overlooked. The attractive chestnut-sided warbler which sings a song sounding very much like its low country cousin, the yellow warbler, likes brushy woods and thickets along the high ridges. Here is a bird benefiting from the coming of man to the American continent, a bird that owes its very abundance to the hand of man. A century or so ago, the bird was so rare that it was almost unknown by pioneer ornithologists such as Audubon who met it only once in his prodigious travels in pursuit of birds. It seems to have existed in small clearings made in the vast forests by fires and blow downs. The clearing of the forests meant a surplus of such habitat and now it is a common bird in areas where it was once unknown. Here is a species aided by man, one to help counterbalance the record of the many species that have suffered.

The lovely Canada warbler is another northerner that finds thickets and rhododendron tangles along streams attractive nesting sites. While afield one August day recently, a chipping sound and jumbled song drew my attention to the brush several yards away. I thought the birds were Canadas, but wanted to see them to be sure. A slate-blue-backed bird with yellow beneath flashed briefly into my field of view which must have been the female. After some contortions on my part for a better view through the thick brush, a yellow breast with black markings, the "necklace" of a male Canada, flashed into sight. This is a bird I always covet seeing and when birding the high ridges seeing and hearing the Canada warbler helps make the day complete.

A bird common in much of the South that makes its summer home in thickets along roads and fields in the valleys of the region is the loggerhead shrike, a songbird with the habits of a hawk. Gray in color with a black mask, the shrike looks a great deal like a mockingbird when it flies and shows white. The shrike is most often seen perched on a wire from which it can survey a large area ready to swoop down on a grasshopper or even a mouse that it will often impale on barbed wire or a thorn until it is ready to eat the morsel. A shrike nests near Franklin and has a favorite perch on an electric line where I have never failed to find it on the many trips I have made by there during the summer. The shrike lingers late into the fall and a few spend the winter when it seems to be more numerous as a winter resident during some years than others.

Another southern bird occasionally seen riding the air currents over the ridges and valleys is the black vulture. This species is distinguished from the larger turkey vulture by its shorter wings and its stump of a tail. The tail of the bigger vulture is characteristically long and not so broad. While the black vulture may nest at a few places in the region, it is most often seen during the late summer and fall when it has drifted northward from points to the south.

The region offers a picture of bird life quite unlike any other part of West Virginia. In the case of a number of species, it is a look at what the bird life was like in other areas a few decades ago. The Bewick's wren is a case in point. Years ago, this wren which is browner than the Carolina wren and shows white in the tail when it flies was a fairly common bird throughout much of the state. Today this is not the case and the bird is entirely absent in areas where it was once found as a nesting species. In Pendleton County and much of the surrounding area, it is still found in numbers around farms where it sings a song that sounds like a buzzing song sparrow and tucks its nest into almost any convenient nook or cranny.

A case similar to that of the Bewick's wren is the lark sparrow. This big sparrow with the reddish pattern on its head, a stickpin on its breast and white in the tail was once found at a number of places in the state, but no more. During the 1963 Brooks Bird Club Foray held in Pendleton County, it was found near the Evick farm on Dickinson Mountain in heavily grazed pastures where clumps of hawthorn were growing and it was here that I saw my first lark sparrows. The Evick farm became a mecca for forayers due to the Bewick's wrens found near the barn and the flock of cliff swallows that had their jug nests plastered to the joists under part of the barn. This swallow is another bird that is found at few other places in the state.

The upper Potomac region is about the only part of the state where the red-headed woodpecker has a status beyond "rare." One summer I had an interesting experience with this species when I saw one flying over the road on Snowy Mountain in Pendleton County on July 10th and on August 27th saw what may have been the same bird flying over the road in the same direction at practically the same location. This attractive woodpecker is found at a number of places in Pendleton and neighboring counties. It has been seen at several places in Grant County and there seems to be a locally numerous population near Fisher in Hardy County. It is heartening to find this gorgeous woodpecker that is such a striking sight in flight present in some numbers in at least one section of the state.

Another woodpecker attracting attention due to it being present in good numbers within the region is the big, crow-sized pileated. This is a species that once seemed destined for extinction, but fortunately it bounced back to become a fairly common bird. Seeing this big wood-pecker is always a stirring sight, but one time remaining foremost in my mind was one afternoon in October as I was driving the river road to Romney from Moorefield. Not far from Moorefield, one flew across the road into the woods above the road. I slowed the car as I tried to get a look at the bird before it flew out of the woods, along the road a short distance and back into the trees. As I was driving up the hill not far ahead, the bird flew over the road with its black and white wings and flaming crest flashing against the blue sky. It was a sight that left me almost breathless.

When the days grow longer and all that remains of winter is little more than a ragged edge, there is a stirring in the land as the first signs of spring appear while the last bits of winter fade before the coming season. The long evenings of winter spent in thought and anticipation of the coming of new sights and sounds are over for another year as one stands on the threshold of spring. It is now time to be out in search of those subtle hints that betray the advance of the months of renewed life across the land. Missing the first signs of spring before it bursts forth in all of its glory is like being absent for the opening movements of a symphony.

A flock of more than a hundred evening grosbeaks seen by the highway near Moorefield early in March were taking winter with them as they were on their way to northern nesting grounds. Another flock of about twenty-five grosbeaks at Durgon the same day seemed to indicate a pronounced movement of the species through the region at that particular time. As I watched these robust finches, the thought came to me that a bird student could hardly have expected to see them here a few decades ago. As I drove on, I knew that it could be two years before I would see them again, but even though they will be missed, the respite from the season of which they are a part is welcomed.

It may seem strange that one can look upon the turkey vulture, the big, grotesque bird that feeds on putrid flesh, as a sign of spring. This bird may seem completely out of step with the freshness and vitality of the season, but even so the big bird is as much a sign of spring in the Potomac highlands as is the robin and maybe even more so. A few vultures are probably found in the region throughout the year, but they do not make their appearance in any numbers until the middle and latter part of February. As February becomes March, more and more of them will be seen over the valleys and ridges as they often circle in a funnel of numerous birds over a carcass. Although many people will continue to look for the first robin and cast their vote for it as the harbinger of spring, the big buzzard is an undisputed sign of a new season even though it prefers to deal in last things.

Some might think it fitting to turn to more appropriate birds as encouraging indications that spring is only a short time away. The vast flocks of blackbirds, red-wings, common grackles and cowbirds, sweeping across the fields gurgling, chipping and mewing in early March make many a farmer uneasy as he thinks of the battle he may have to wage with them later in the year when the crops are ready for harvest. The phoebe appears on the scene about the same time, but this gray bird is content to travel alone as it begins looking for a place on a ledge, under a bridge or in a building to place its nest of mud and moss. This sociable flycatcher can be seen perched on a wire bobbing its tail and calling its name before sallying forth to snatch an insect.

Then there is the robin that puts life into a warm evening in March as it takes its stand on a rooftop and pours forth its clear notes in the fading daylight. I cannot decide whether it is the bird that gives charm to the season or the season that adds charm to the song of the robin, but perhaps this is only a needless inquiry on my part. It is easy to understand why the robin means spring and if you prefer, vice versa. On a warm evening that calls the robin to perform, the chorus of the frogs down by the pond, the fresh smell on the light breeze, also add to the essence of spring, that certain something not easily defined in words, but which has its very content in all of these.

One morning late in March as I sat at breakfast dozing, I was brought to alertness by the singing of a Bewick's wren from the field not far from the house. The evening of the same day, I saw a Bewick's wren near Petersburg. A buzzing song drew my attention to the wren singing near a shed. As I walked towards the bird, it scolded as it dodged through the bushes along a fence. The Bewick's wren was back and it was no doubt returning to many other sheds to build its nest.

On an afternoon in early April while driving up the North Fork near Riverton, I brought the car to a stop when I saw six ducks on a farm pond. Immediately I knew they were scaups because the males were "black on both ends and white in the middle." There were four males and two females peacefully dozing as they drifted on the water completely oblivious to the fact that I was spying on them from the road. The scaup is characteristically a duck of the bays, lakes and estuaries and is one of the most common species of its kind and if one is going to see a diver anywhere, it will most likely be a scaup.

Needless to say, in this mountainous country of swiftly flowing rivers seeing the scaups was a noteworthy event. I have often wondered how the South Branch River got its Indian name which is said to mean "river of wild geese." If this is indeed what the word means, it seems inconceivable that even in former times when there was a greater abundance of waterfowl that geese would occur in any numbers on the river. Could it be that the opposite was true? The occurrence of geese on the river was so rare that it was an event long remembered when it did occur and the river was given its name by the Indians out of these circumstances.

As I was driving along feeling fortunate for having passed by while the scaups were resting before cleaving the air out of the mountains, I saw four ducks on another pond. As I took a closer look, I found two male and one female blue-winged teals along with a male scaup that dived several times while I watched before it bobbed back to the surface. The teal is identified by the white crescent on the face of the male and, in flight, by the chalky blue that the bird shows in its wings and hence its name.

.

Fig. 25. While it is possible with some luck to find a screech owl feigning a dead limb in an effort to camouflage itself, the little owl will most often be heard during the late summer and fall when they become vociferous.

Another record of note had been made and I began wondering what had forced these ducks down. No doubt they had been flying over the mountains and ran head long into the front of foul weather passing over the region and dropped down to find respite on the first water they found. The same evening, I saw a pied-billed grebe on the river near Upper Tract. A grebe is an archaic thing whose ancestors ornithologists speculate may have helped span the bridge between reptiles and birds, but even so it is a water bird and was a welcomed sight. I did not realize it at the time, but the next several days were to prove that perhaps the South Branch had rightfully earned its Indian name.

While on my way to join a group of birders from Franklin on Saturday morning, I saw a pair of wood ducks on the river and the bright colors on the male seemed to shine on the water like the rainbow hues in a pool of oil as it dances on the surface. A few kingfishers were seen along the river as they fished and scolded with their rattling chatter, but we stopped along the river only briefly before we reached the small marsh near Upper Tract. I tramped through the high, brown grass and the cattails while the others watched from the road and kicked up several snipes and a black-crowned night heron.

On the way to Fort Seybert where we hoped to find some waterfowl on the ponds in that area, we found a screech owl roosting in a small white pine. On one of the large flood control reservoirs near

Fort Seybert we found a number of ducks. We counted six buffle-
heads, the attractive little duck with a large patch of white on the
male's head that almost seems to ride and bob on the water like a
bathtub toy. Four pairs of hooded mergansers were some distance
out on the water and the fan-shaped crests on the males were closed
and looked merely like streaks of gray hair along the sides of their
heads. A pair of scaups and two blue-winged teals were also present
on the lake.

The best was yet to come as far as waterfowl were concerned
when several hundred ducks and gulls descended on the sewage disposal
pond at Franklin during the following week when the weather had really
gone foul with rain, snow and fog. A sewage disposal pond may seem a
rather inhospitable place to observe water birds, but the one at Franklin is quite odor free and from all outward appearances merely looks
like a rectangular pond.

Nearly a dozen loons were present in this large aggregation of
water birds and they looked quite stream-lined as they swam back and
forth across the pond and dived, but this almost seemed a show to
cover the insecurity they feel on land where they are quite clumsy. A
loon confined to the land is almost a doomed bird because it must have
water surface across which to paddle in order to get itself airborne.
Occasionally, one of the birds would wail its strange call which is one
of the sounds of the northern wilderness which has given that area
much of its romance and legends. The demoniac wailing of the bird is
also the source of the expression that a mentally deranged person is as
crazy as a loon. I would suppose that a loon is really quite mentally
sound or as rational as a bird can be. For a few brief days, the wailing of the loons became one of the sounds along the upper Potomac
where the bird may seem a bit out of place without a backdrop of
spruce and the crystal waters of a northern lake to glide across, but
even though it was forced to condescend to a sewage disposal pond it
was a welcomed sight.

Along with a couple of hundred scaups that were riding the
surface of the pond, there were several red-breasted mergansers
with their ragged crests and a dozen ruddy ducks. The male ruddy
is a cocky fellow that often swims with his tail fanned that gives him
the appearance of a diminuitive turkey cock strutting. Nearly five
hundred gulls came down on the pond and in the surrounding fields
and most of these were the rather nondescript and common herring
gull, but about fifty of the black-headed Bonaparte's gulls were also
present. Later in the week, a single Bonaparte's gull was seen on a
small pond that was little more than a water hole near Fort Seybert.
The bird seemed lost and forlorn so far from the coast as I watched
it swimming about in the muddy water with thirsty cows standing about.

The peak of bird migration in the spring occurs in early May and to miss spending at least one day in the field at this time is to miss skimming the cream off of the milk of the season. Bird enthusiasts across the country look forward with eager anticipation to that day in May when they will test their skill at sight and sound identification in an effort to tally over one hundred bird species. The competition has grown very keen between bird clubs in many cities and counties and while the effort is made to see and hear as many birds as possible during a twenty-four hour period, there is also the incentive to top the number seen by a rival club. The day is known by various titles across the country such as Century Day, Big Day or May Day, but it all means an all-out effort to find at least, if not more than, one hundred bird species in a day.

Saturday, May 7, was only seconds old when I heard the whippoor-will and the day was off to a good start with the first bird on the list recorded without leaving the house. I went to bed in order to get a few hours sleep before getting up before daylight in an effort to hear owls before they quieted down with the coming of daylight. About 2:30 a. m. I woke up and in a few minutes heard a barred owl calling from the woods at the edge of town. It had almost been as though my subconscious was telling me to wake up because there was a bird to add to the list. I decided this was about as good as I could expect to do before daylight since I had these two luxury items on the list and I reset the alarm for six in order to get a little more sleep than what I had originally planned.

I met the others in Franklin shortly after seven and the list began to grow as we added yellow warbler, purple martin and goldfinch in town while the brown thrasher, cardinal and orchard oriole were tallied in the thickets along the road. We walked down to the sewage disposal pond where we saw a few spotted sandpipers after we had checked off a boisterous kingbird and the meadowlark.

We drove through the cemetery where we made several important additions to the list. A yellow-breasted chat was seen hopping about in a small bush before dropping to the ground. In the hemlocks we heard the songs of warblers and intently watched for movement in order to pick the birds out. I saw a burst of yellow which proved to be the breast of the magnolia warbler. A song that sounded somewhat like that of the yellow warbler belonged to the chestnut-sided warbler. Myrtle warblers were also present with their yellow rump patches clearly identifying them when they flew. We heard the slurred song of a yellow-throated vireo and the buzzing of a golden-winged warbler came from a brushy field. A white-crowned sparrow was feeding in the grass before it flew up to perch on a tombstone. The attractive sparrow was the last bird tallied before we were on the road again.

On the way down the river, a stop at the mill race near an old saw mill did not prove very profitable when we found only a phoebe and heard the rattling of a kingfisher along the river. The buzzing and trilling notes we heard from the woods near Ruddle brought us to a stop as we pulled the car off the road and got out to see what we could add to the list.

A red-breasted nuthatch was scrambling about on the limbs and cones of a pine. A thrill of delight shot through all of us when we saw the Blackburnian warbler with its flaming throat. A bird dangling from the end of a pine branch with a bluish back having an olive patch was the parula warbler. A redstart was fluttering about among the branches while the myrtle warblers were singing at a number of places in the treetops. A black and white warbler was seen creeping along a limb before we heard its mousy notes. The song of a wood thrush came from the distant woods.

The burst of new birds for the list had run its course and we were on the road again. We stopped at the small marsh near Upper Tract which yielded only a swamp sparrow before driving into the mountains towards Deer Run.

We spotted a pair of wood ducks on a pool in a small stream before they flew a short distance to land in a hickory. Even the male in his gorgeous plumage blended so well with the background that only by scrutinizing the tree with our binoculars could the pair be seen. The iridescent green on the head of the male and the red on the cheek shone brightly in the morning sun.

A short distance from where the ducks were seen, four bob-whites were stealing across shaly ground through a patch of prickly pear cactus. How appropriate to see the quail in the cactus where they animated this bit of western flora. In the West, a few species of quails are found in the rocky, cactus country.

While driving up the mountain through the woods, we heard the song of a rose-breasted grosbeak. Soon the beautiful male came into view in the lightly leaved trees accompanied by the rather drab female. After watching the grosbeaks for a short time, we found ourselves in the midst of a number of other birds.

A crested flycatcher cried wheeep! from the woods. We heard the zray, zray, zray, zreee of a cerulean warbler and the weak buzz of a worm-eating warbler. An ovenbird was seen in the bushes near the road. Myrtle warblers were singing and flitting about in the trees practically all around us. The black-throated blue and black-throated green warblers soon added their lazy notes to the medley of warbler songs. A rather discordant note was added to the whole affair when the harsh croak of a raven came from across the mountain. The clear weta-weta-we-teo of a hooded warbler added another warbler to the list. A Canada warbler was seen and heard in a laurel thicket near where the hooded was singing. This bonanza of warblers was completed by the Nashville warbler we saw and heard singing its well-defined notes that end in a jumble.

A red-headed woodpecker was flying across a field showing a great deal of white which is a characteristic mark of this woodpecker in flight. After it landed, we studied it closely breathing in the sight of the beautiful plumage which looks like a piece torn from the American flag and knowing this might be the only one we would see during the day.

As we rounded a curve shortly after seeing the woodpecker, two birds flew up from the ground that showed white in their tails. As I looked at them closely, all of the marks fell into place--white in the tail, stickpin on the breast and a reddish pattern on the head. They were lark sparrows! What an attractive sparrow and, in my mind, they are surpassed in beauty only by the white-crowned sparrow. The vagabond nature of the lark sparrow, its here today, gone tomorrow existence over the years within the state has given it a special attractiveness to all who search for it. We watched them as they flew from one place to another until they had disappeared across the ridge.

We were lucky to see what might be called two of the Pendleton County specialities, the red-headed woodpecker and the lark sparrow, within such a short distance of each other. We were then on our way to find another, the cliff swallow, at an abandoned farm. A solitary sandpiper on each of the two water holes at the farm seemed so incongruous in the upland setting, but they were a valuable addition to the list. A few of the swallows flying around the big barn and over the nearby pond were cliff swallows which were identified by their pale rump patches. Barn swallows were also about that had their nests in the barn and rough-winged swallows were seen over the pond.

Before crossing the mountain to Fort Seybert and with eighty-five species on the list, we made use of a picnic table at the Deer Run Methodist Church since the time was now past noon. While we ate our sandwiches, we listened to Baltimore orioles and vesper sparrows and watched the red-wings frolicking in the fields.

Shortly after crossing the mountain, we saw a large hawk circling over the valley. The rufous on the tail tagged it a red-tailed hawk as it rose higher in its circling. With a rush of great wings, a turkey vulture flew up from the road only a short distance in front of the car and perched in a tree. We watched the big bird with its naked, ugly head for a minute or two before it flew out of sight. We wondered what the attraction was that made the buzzard reluctant to leave and found our answer in the putrid carcass of a woodchuck over which flies were buzzing.

Not far from Fort Seybert, we found a small flock of white-throated sparrows in a hemlock near a farmhouse. Near the river, we heard the rollicking tea-kettle, tea-kettle, tea-kettle, tea of a Carolina wren and saw the green heron. The savannah sparrow was added to the list when it was the only bird we found in a small marsh other than some swamp sparrows which had already been listed. A grasshopper sparrow gave us a good opportunity to watch it as it perched on a fence and sang its jumbled song which is less often heard than its insect-like buzz.

From Fort Seybert, it was up the river to Sugar Grove where we saw a loggerhead shrike as we began the drive across the southern end of the county. I glimpsed a bird flying into a clump of hawthorn which I thought was a shrike instead of a mockingbird. When the bird flew out and perched in full view it proved to be a shrike. A hawk perched in the top of a large oak nearby was identified as a red-tail when it flew.

Not far from route 220, a female scaup duck was found on a small pond. With the duck being the 94th bird on the list, we crossed Snowy Mountain on our way into Pocahontas County to Gaudineer Knob where we would end the day by seeing what birds we could find in the spruce.

It was early in the evening when we arrived at the stand of virgin spruce on Shaver's Mountain and few birds were active. A few juncos were singing their ringing notes and we saw a few as they flew up through the woods with their tails flashing white in the darkened spruce. Soon a small bird flew into the top of a tree near a Blackburnian warbler that we had been watching and it proved to be a solitary vireo. The bubbling, rollicking song of a winter wren came from the spruce down the mountain.

Very few birds were present in the spruce around the fire tower on the knob. The sky was clear and the view was unobstructed in all directions. In the distance, we could see the crest of Spruce Knob and the long ridge of Spruce Mountain. I heard and saw a golden-crowned kinglet as it sang its weak, wiry notes in the darkening spruce below the tower.

On the way from the knob to the main highway, we saw a ruffed grouse perched in a tree. By the highway on our way to Red Run to find the Northern waterthrush, we saw another grouse and heard a winter wren. A short time after arriving at Red Run, we heard the waterthrush singing from the swamp.

Back at the Pocahontas Restaurant we had a snack before driving to Franklin. It was now past dark and as we stepped outside, we heard the nasal call of a woodcock and soon heard its bubbling and whistling as it was doing its sky dance over the spruce near the high-

Fig. 26. A common game bird in the region is the ruffed grouse which may be encountered as it flies away with the whir of wings as it springs from the forest floor or heard when its drumming fills the air with a thumping sound.

way. We listened to its performance for awhile before checking it off as the 100th bird of the day and leaving for Franklin.

The most interesting aspect of the bird life during the summer months within the region is the number of species that can be found along the higher ridges and mountains which are characteristic or common birds of the North or of the Canadian spruce forests. These birds are found in few other regions within the state and are absent as summer residents at the lower elevations.

In Pendleton County, the high ridges of Spruce Mountain, North Fork Mountain and Shenandoah Mountain offer conditions of forest types and climate that are favored by these various northern species. It is only along the high, long ridge of Spruce Mountain and along the western edge of the county that the most boreal and Canadian conditions of plant life and various ecological factors are found in Pendleton County in that this is the only area where spruce grows. While this is the case and a number of species are confined to this area with its northern aspects, others are not as demanding in the environmental conditions they require and are found along most of the higher ridges in the county.

Reddish Knob offers a good cross sectional view of the northern birds found within the county during the summer months when birds are occupied with the defense of territories and the raising of young. The elevation at Reddish Knob is about 4400 feet and while there is no spruce at the knob, a number of birds can be found there and along the higher slopes of Shenandoah Mountain that are found at only the higher elevations in Pendleton County.

The drive to Reddish Knob is interesting in that as one notes the plant life along the way, it is possible to note a marked change in the vegetation, as well as in the bird life, as one goes higher up the mountain. As one begins the drive from near Sugar Grove, the road passes through dry woods of oak and pine where scrub oak and bracken make up much of the underbrush in the woods. In some of the abandoned fields that are growing up with pines one may hear the prairie warbler singing its ascending notes and hear the buzzing notes of the golden-winged warbler. The worm-eating warbler and blue-gray gnatcatcher will be found in the dry woods where the soil has been worn down from Devonian shale.

Higher up the slopes of the mountain, the forest takes on a different character and it is also at this point that the bird life assumes a different nature. At an elevation of about 3000 feet where such trees as basswood, cucumbertree, yellow birch and butternut make their appearance and often grow to impressive sizes in some of the shaded ravines, the black-throated green warbler will be heard singing its lazy notes. Even though this bird can be found in the county at slightly lower elevations in somewhat different forest conditions, on Shenandoah Mountain it seems to serve as a good key species to indicate a different forest type and a new zone of bird life. Soon the black-throated blue warbler will be heard and this species is undeniably a bird of the high elevations.

The jumbled song of the Canada warbler will come from the dense growth of laurel near the road where this striking warbler with its bright yellow breast has found the abundance of laurel much to its liking and several may be heard as one approaches the crest of the mountain. The solitary vireo sings from the woods and sounds somewhat like a slow and lazy red-eyed vireo while juncos will be seen flying up from the edge of the road with their white tail feathers snapping like scissors.

As I was driving to Reddish Knob one summer day, a raven flew from some large rocks by the road as I rounded a curve and I was able to watch it for some time as it rode the air currents while drifting down the ridge. The chestnut-sided warblers were singing from the brush around the fire tower when I arrived at the knob late in the morning.

After leaving the knob, about halfway down the mountain my attention was attracted to a song that was strange to me coming from the pines by the road. I looked through the pines until I saw a bird perched which proved to be a male red crossbill after I had studied it closely through the binoculars. The heavy bill of the bird made it look like a small, red parrot. The bird sang two more times at the same perch before flying up to feed on the seeds of cones of the table mountain pine. Soon I saw a female in one of the pines and another male flew into one of the pines momentarily before flying out of sight. I watched the first male for several minutes as it moved about feeding and resting from time to time. I am certain other crossbills were in the immediate vicinity because shortly after I saw the first bird, I heard the call notes of others down the slope, but the only ones that I saw were the three. It came as a real surprise to find crossbills in pines near Reddish Knob because I thought I could expect to find them only along Spruce Mountain where I might find them with some luck.

The following day on the way to Spruce Knob Lake and Spruce Knob, I drove to the stand of virgin hemlock and northern hardwoods near Cherry Grove in an effort to see if this tract of timber harbored birds which would usually be found at the highest elevations. Two magnolia warblers were heard singing and it seems that this species is found widespread at the higher elevations in a host of forest types from the pure northern hardwoods to hemlock-hardwood associations and pure stands of spruce. The high, thin song of a Blackburnian warbler was heard coming from high in a hemlock. Several black-throated greens and black-throated blues were singing and, near the road, a parula warbler buzzed upward in its singing.

I left the tract of virgin timber and drove towards the lake. In the spruce-hardwood forests not far from the lake, I heard black-throated greens, juncos and magnolia warblers. I found a swamp sparrow in a marshy area at the shallow end of the lake and saw a few solitary vireos in the woods near the lake. I heard the black-throated blue warbler and two Canada warblers as I was leaving the lake.

On the way to the knob from the lake, my attention was attracted to a golden-crowned kinglet singing its high notes that end in a chickadee-like chatter from a stand of spruce. The small bird was moving about in the spruce as it sang and was hidden from view by the thick branches. I followed the bird by its song as it moved about until it came into sight near the end of a limb. When it bent forward while foraging on the limb, the light struck it and I could clearly see the orange on its striped crown. This little bird is truly a resident of the spruce and is found where the spruce has grown back in stands where the trees are several inches in diameter now that the land has had many years to recuperate from the lumbering days.

Fig. 27. The song of the wood thrush is one of the most enchanting sounds in the summer woods at all elevations and the stirring
songs of its close relatives, the Swainson's thrush and veery, can be
heard at the high elevations where these species add to the richness
of bird life.

From a rocky expanse beneath the trees near the road came
the bubbling, gurgling and trilling song of a winter wren. This little
brown sprite seems to prefer rocky places where it can play hide and
seek among the boulders or bounce through the air on a momentary
flight from one boulder to another. The song of the winter wren sounds
all out of proportion to the size of the bird and it is a real wonder how
such energy and exuberance can be packed into such a small bundle of
feathers. It seems almost as though the winter wren has taken a buzz
or a trill from the songs of the other wrens and set them to a slightly
different tune to come up with its long and sustained song.

The warbling of a purple finch came from near the top of a
spruce while nearby a rose-breasted grosbeak was perched in a maple
near the road. The bright, rosy patch on the bird's breast seemed to
dance like a flame on the limb as the grosbeak moved about. This is a
beautiful bird in flight when it shows black mingled with white and the
rose of its breast.

The ethereal notes of a Swainson's thrush came from the woods
near the road and the notes seemed so light and airy that they floated
upward on the air. Other Swainson's thrushes joined in and the woods
were filled with a chorus of airy and other-worldly songs. A veery

added its beautiful song to the chorus that was in progress with the notes of the veery spiraling downward. The song of the veery, in my mind, is one of the most stirring and haunting sounds of nature and it is a song that can be heard only at the higher elevations and in the spruce woods during the summer. The chorus of the thrushes ceased almost as rapidly as it had started and the woods were still again except for a breeze that occasionally rustled the leaves.

A number of widespread and common species were found near the knob. The blue jays were calling loudly from the woods and a yellowthroat sang from the brush near the road. The yellowthroat is found rather commonly is brushy places at the higher elevations in the western part of Pendleton County, but is much less common at the lower elevations where much of the land is kept cleared or is closely grazed and there is little brush land suitable for the bird. Catbirds and brown thrashers were present in the brush and a raven called harshly from off along the mountain.

As I arrived at the knob, a towhee was singing and this species is found from the lowest to the highest elevations during the summer months. The juncos were singing their notes that sound like the ringing of a small, delicate bell from the stunted spruce while a purple finch offered its song from the dwarfed trees near the parking area close to the highest point of land in West Virginia.

A red-tailed hawk was circling off the ridge as I was leaving the knob. I thought I heard crossbills in the spruce by the road and as I watched, two red crossbills flew over and down the slope out of sight. I certainly would have never thought that two days in a row I would get the red crossbill on each side of the county. I had a feeling that it would take a lot of luck and a great deal of time to do it again.

As I drove down the mountain, I thought how the past two days had been a good look at the birds that are found at the higher elevations in the county during the summer months. I had seen and heard the black-throated green and black-throated blue warblers that almost seem to sing their songs halfheartedly and wistfully from the hardwood forests along the higher ridges and also from the spruce woods along Spruce Mountain. The solitary vireo that wears a blue hood and white spectacles had been found at the high places where it sings its song that suggests the more common and widespread red-eyed vireo. The Blackburnian warbler with its flaming throat was present in the large hemlocks where the virgin timber stood and its high song had also been heard in the spruce and hardwoods along Spruce Mountain. The juncos with their gray plumage which is given some mark of distinction by the white tail feathers when they fly were seen and heard at Reddish Knob and at many places from the lake to the highest point in the state. The chestnut-sided warblers, a rare species a century ago, were rather common in the thickets where it sings a song that is suggestive of the yellow warbler. The Canada warbler with its bright yellow breast that has a necklace of black spots sang from a number of laurel thickets from Reddish Knob and at high points towards Spruce Knob. The attractive magnolia warbler had been found in the virgin timber and in the spruce and hardwood forests around the lake and towards the knob. The rose-breasted grosbeak had lent its enchanting beauty to the host of birds found at the higher elevations. The Swainson's thrush and veery had added their haunting songs to the sounds that were heard on the way to Spruce Knob.

A few species had been found that are restricted to Spruce Mountain and the patches of spruce that grow along its slopes. The long, exuberant song of the winter wren had been heard here as this little bird makes its home in a number of similar situations along the high, spruce-capped ridges the length of the Appalachians. The golden-crowned kinglet had been heard and seen in the spruce woods where it nests and shuns other types of habitat. The purple finch with its blush of rosy plumage had been found in patches of spruce and it seems to need spruce trees before it will settle down for the summer. Last, but certainly not least, there had been the red crossbills that I had found near Reddish Knob and at Spruce Knob. This bird with its transient existence never really seems to settle down and stay in one place for long. Even though it has been found in the red spruce at a number of places in West Virginia during the summer months, no nest has ever been found. The very vagabond and unpredictable nature of the bird was pointed out by the fact that I found it near Reddish Knob where there is no spruce and where it would not be expected.

The red crossbill serves as a prime example to point out an aspect of the bird life of the Potomac highlands and this is that the birds may not always play by the rules as far as distribution and habitat are concerned. One who keeps in close touch with the bird life of the region may find that the unexpected may become rather common-place and the unusual can often seem like the rule rather than the exception. In short, one who searches for birds in the upper Potomac area will find many rewards for his efforts and there will be few dull moments as he follows the ebb and flow of wings over the mountains.

APPENDIX ONE

SOURCES AND ACKNOWLEDGMENTS

The curiosity of a reader may prompt him to ask of a writer the question of what has prompted the writing of a book, but an author may not answer this question in the book itself. If anyone has asked this question of the present writer, the answer follows.

My interest in the upper Potomac area was whetted while I was a student at West Virginia University. In various classes of botany and zoology as the professors made reference to the interesting and even unusual aspects of the plant and animal life at the headwaters of the Potomac River, my thoughts were stirred and I began to dream dreams as though they were talking about some exotic and distant land. My introduction to the area came during botany and geology field trips to a number of the more interesting and outstanding areas of botanical and geological interest in Grant County.

This brief introduction to the riches of the region merely whetted my appetite for more and during 1963 I spent more than a week in Pendleton County at the Brooks Bird Club Foray. During that time, my interest in the area was deepened by the fact that I was responsible for compiling and editing the list of birds that were observed during the foray. The bird life of the county needed further study and investigation as a result of many of the interesting records that were compiled during the foray. On leaving the county at the end of the foray, I decided that when the first opportunity presented itself I would return in order to learn more about the natural history of the county that had become a part of my very being. I had no idea at that time that the course of events in my life during the next two years would make it possible for me to return and spend the entire year as a resident of the area while serving as a Methodist minister.

The Potomac Naturalist had its beginning during the "Blizzard of '66." While a seminary student in Washington, D.C. and carrying out preaching and parish responsibilities on the weekends, I became snow-bound in Washington during the last days of January, 1966. Much of the East was immobilized by the heavy snow that fell during that weekend and I jokingly say that I had nothing better to do than to start writing a book, but that is essentially what I did. For some months, I had been thinking about writing a paper on the natural aspects of the upper Potomac and turned to the typewriter where I rather hastily composed a page of notes that was the skeleton of what was to grow into The Potomac Naturalist.

With no references to turn to and with little research undertaken, instead of beginning at the beginning, I started at the end and began the chapter on bird life since this was the phase of the natural history that I was most familiar with and could draw from my own experiences. Considering the weather during that weekend, it seems like a pun to say that the undertaking snowballed, but that is what happened. As time went on, I found more information that I wanted to include and the undertaking became the writing of a book.

The upper Potomac highlands have a story that has needed telling for many years and I have attempted to tell that story. The reader in his own judgment will decide whether or not I have been successful.

An author could be defined as a person who has the time to compile a number of articles, draw material from a number of books and present his efforts in an undertaking of book length. Numerous people in the past who recorded their observations of historical events, the geology, the plant and animal life of the upper Potomac region have had a part in the writing of this book and without their past efforts it could have never been written. While most information has been taken from written sources, a number of people have contributed a great deal of information through their conversations with me and their sharing of events that are recorded in their memories.

The present book is a compilation, assimilation and distillation of many books, articles and records that have been written and compiled over the years. If anyone would want to pursue any aspect of the history and natural history of the region at the headwaters of the Potomac River, he can find more detailed information in the following sources.

A number of persons have assisted me in many ways in the preparation and writing of this book. The mentioning of their names along with the sources that have been used at the end of this work certainly is not intended to minimize the valuable contribution that these persons have made in aiding me in this undertaking.

Any author who searches for a picture in historical writings of the appearance of the landscape of an area at the time of settlement usually has a difficult task confronting him. Through references to a number of sources and from a piece of information from one book and a bit of information from another reference, it becomes possible to put together a picture of the wildlife, forests, Indian inhabitants and other aspects of the land at the time of the appearance of the first settlers on the scene.

Oren Morton's History of Pendleton County (Ruebush-Elkins Co., Dayton, Va., 1910) has been a valuable source of information for a number of reasons in reference to the early history of the region. His discussion of the early Indian dwellers of the area as well as accounts of the attacks on the frontier forts at Upper Tract and Fort Seybert have been particularly valuable. Few historical writers have recorded information on the wilderness scene, but fortunately Morton has recorded records of bounty payments made in Pendleton County along with a few valuable notes on the wildlife of the area at the time of settlement.

Other information on the Indians in the region and area archeology, particularly in reference to Old Fields, was found in A History of the Valley of Virginia by Samuel Kercheval (4th edition, Shenandoah Publishing Co., Strasburg, Va., 1925). This book also provided the most extensive account of the heroic deeds of Samuel Bingamon and information on the Fairfax lands.

L. Virgil McWhorter's Border Settlers of Northwestern Virginia (Republican Publishing Co., Hamilton, Ohio, 1915) has served as a valuable reference for notes on mammals that are no longer found in the state and upper Potomac region.

I turned to the story of the life of Meshach Browning in order to find accounts of his probable visits to the region. Forty-four Years of the Life of a Hunter, Meshach Browning (J. P. Lippincott & Co., Phila., 1859) is an account of the hunting trips and heroic deeds of the great Maryland hunter.

The most valuable list of West Virginia mammals is "An Annotated List of West Virginia Mammals" by Remington Kellogg in the Proceedings of the U. S. National Museum (84:443–479. 1937). This list contains notes on the mammals that were collected within the state by a party from the museum and it also has information on the status of all mammals known in West Virginia up to that time. I prize highly a copy of this list that I was able to obtain from a dealer in used and rare books.

Mammals of Eastern United States by William Hamilton, Jr. (Comstock Publishing Co., Ithaca, N.Y., 1943) and The Mammal Guide by Ralph S. Palmer (Doubleday & Co., Garden City, N.Y., 1954) have frequently been consulted for information on the habits, color and length of various mammals.

Zina Cosner of Bismarck supplied me with much valuable information on wolves, mountain lions and the passenger pigeon in that part of Grant County. Harrison Shobe, retired conservation officer for Grant County, was helpful by referring me to various people in my search for information. I would also express thanks to many hunters and old-timers who had no idea that anything they said might find its way into the pages of this book.

Anyone who looks for an account of the geological history of a region that can be read and easily understood by a layman is probably in for a futile search. Most discussions of the geology of a particular area are written by professional geologists and are shot full of the jargon and technical terms in which this professionally trained person speaks. I have tried to piece together a picture of the geology of the upper Potomac that can be read and understood by anyone who is interested in learning something about the processes involved in forming the mountains and valleys with all of their many geological facets.

The most valuable reference has been The Geology and Natural Resources of West Virginia by Price, Tucker and Haught (Vol. X, W. Va. Geological Survey, 1938). This reference supplied me with information on the geological history of West Virginia that had particular application to the three county area. The discussion of the various eras, periods and rock structures were most helpful in piecing together the geology of the upper Potomac.

For recent information on the investigations into the igneous rocks that are found in Pendleton County, Igneous Rocks of Pendleton County, West Virginia, by Thomas E. Garner, Jr. (Report of Investigations No. 12, W. Va. Geological Survey, Morgantown, 1956) has been a valuable reference.

In order to gain an understanding of the geosynclinal idea of the formation of the Appalachians, I turned to The Evolution of North America by Philip B. King (Princeton University Press, Princeton, N. J., 1959). This author's discussion of the geological history of the mid-Appalachians is very good and gave me a framework in which to build an account of the events in the three county area.

The most valuable source of information on the formation, history and descriptions of the caves and caverns in the region is Caverns of West Virginia by William E. Davies (Vol. XIX, W. Va. Geological Survey, 1949) and its 1965 supplement which contains information on the location and description of caves discovered since the publication of this volume. Once a person has mastered the terms that are used in this book, it is an invaluable guide to the underground world of caves in West Virginia.

Information on the visit of Francis Asbury to Stratosphere Balloon Cave was taken from the account found in Asbury's Journal (N. Bangs & T. Mason, New York, 1821). Notes on the exploration of Schoolhouse Cave were taken from Exploring American Caves by Franklin Folsom (Collier Books, New York, N.Y., 1962). This book is a good source for anyone interested in the overall view of the geology, history and lore associated with many caves in America.

I want to express my appreciation to Dr. Alan Donaldson, Geology Department, West Virginia University, who read the manuscript on geology and made many valuable comments and criticisms in order that I could make a few corrections and alterations prior to publication. I want to thank Estyl Lambert of Seneca Caverns for allowing me to enter Stratosphere Balloon Cave and the managers of Smokehole Caverns for the courtesy they extended me during my visit to the caverns. Linton Sites of Petersburg accompanied me on a number of spelunking endeavors and allowed me to borrow caving gear. The A. L. Nesselrodts were very courteous in allowing me and my cohorts in caving to enter Kenny Simmons' Cave.

One of the most valuable sources for gaining information on the original appearance of the forests along the Allegheny Front is H. A. Allard and E. C. Leonard's "The Canaan and Stony River Valleys in West Virginia, etc., " Castanea 17:1-60. This paper is an effort to reconstruct the appearance of the original spruce forests in these areas along with a discussion of the Pleistocene glaciation and its influence on the formation of the forests and the presence of northern flora.

Frequent reference has been made to "The Vascular Flora of the Monongahela National Forest, West Virginia, " by Roy Clarkson in Castanea 31:1-120. This reference has been an important source of information for a discussion of the original forest conditions, the destruction of the forests by lumbering and fire, notes on the "balds" found in the region and comments on plants that are found at various places. Tumult on the Mountains (McClain Printing Co., Parsons, 1964) by the same author has been a good source for information on the original forest conditions and the lumbering industry.

For its historical value in its discussion of the appearance of the forests about the turn of the century, A. B. Brooks' Forestry and Wood Industries (Vol. V, W.Va. Geological Survey, 1911) has been consulted frequently. This reference has particular value historically for its treatment of the forests at the time of the author's field work in the region during 1908.

For notes on the lives of various botanists, I turned to Life and Writings of Rafinesque by R. E. Call (1895) and "Hamilton McSparrin Gamble" by Patty Chrisman, Castanea 19:21-24, is the most detailed account of the life of the Moorefield physician and botanist that is available. Notes on the life of Moses Bennett were gleaned from Weldon Boone's History of Botany in West Virginia (McClain Printing Co.,

1965) and this book was a valuable source for information on the shale barren endemics and the botanists who discovered them.

The best discussion of the flora of the shale barrens is Earl L. Core's "Shale Barren Flora of West Virginia" in the Proceedings of the W. Va. Academy of Science (14:27-36). This article has information on the discovery and description of these plants along with notes on their known distribution up to 1940. Core's "Ranges of Some Plants on the Appalachian Shale Barrens, " Castanea 17:105-116, served as a supplement to the preceding article for its more recent information on the distribution of the endemics.

The Masters theses of Norlyn Bodkin, The Vascular Flora of Pendleton County, West Virginia, (West Virginia University, Morgantown, 1962) and Carroll Clark's The Vascular Flora of Grant County, West Virginia, (West Virginia University, Morgantown, 1964) have been helpful for notes on the distribution of various plants in these two counties.

The most valuable source of information on the description and range of plants found in West Virginia is without a doubt Flora of West Virginia by P. D. Strausbaugh and Earl L. Core which appeared in four volumes from 1952 through 1964 as Bulletins of West Virginia University. Numerous references have been made to these volumes for descriptions, ranges, the discoverers and describers of many plants found within the state. Core's Vegetation of West Virginia (McClain Printing Co., Parsons, 1966) is a good reference to bring many phases of the plant life of the state into focus.

The Wild Flower Guide by Edgar T. Wherry (Doubleday & Co., 1948) and this author's Fern Guide (Doubleday & Co., 1961) have been helpful for notes on the descriptions and distribution of various plants.

Miss Elizabeth Ann Bartholomew of the West Virginia University Herbarium has been very courteous in allowing me to examine specimens contained in the herbarium collection and assisting me in my search for information on the plant life of the upper Potomac. I want especially to thank Dr. Earl L. Core for taking time from his busy schedule to discuss with me various aspects of the flora of the upper Potomac region and to read the manuscript on plants and check it for accuracy.

Most of the information on the bird life has been gained through my own field work, but I am indebted to various authors for information. Hawks Aloft (Dodd, Mead & Co., New York, N.Y., 1949) by Maurice Broun has been a valuable reference for its discussion of the migration of birds of prey and the status of the golden eagle in the East.

The Appalachians (Houghton Mifflin Co., Boston, 1965) by Maurice Brooks contains information on the bird life of the region particularly in reference to the golden eagle and this author's A Check-List of West Virginia Birds (Agr. Exp. Station, Morgantown, 1944) has been referred to a great number of times for notes on the status of various birds in the state and Potomac region.

I want to thank a number of people who have accompanied me in the field on a number of occasions and have been helpful to me as I have gathered information on the bird life. Carolyn and Mary Lee Ruddle of Franklin have given attention to the bird life of that area and have passed many valuable notes on to me. Without the sharp eyes of several young people many birds would have been overlooked and I want to thank Leslie Jo Wilfong, Danny Bill Landis, Barbara and Lucille Brown, John Dorsey and Chuck Byers whose companionship in the field has made many a day a fun-filled adventure.

APPENDIX TWO

A LIST OF SCIENTIFIC NAMES

A variety of common names may be used in reference to a certain plant and since common names come and go in popular usage the following list of the Latin names of the plants mentioned in the main text is intended to be of assistance in determining the exact species to which a reference is made. The nomenclature is drawn from Flora of West Virginia by P. D. Strausbaugh and Earl L. Core which follows the 8th Edition of Gray's Manual of Botany (1950).

Rue Spleenwort (Asplenium cryptolepis)
Black-stem Spleenwort (Asplenium resiliens)
Purple Cliffbrake (Pellaea atropurpurea)
Hairy Lip Fern (Cheilanthes lanosa)
Maidenhair Fern (Adiantum pedatum)
Bracken (Pteridium aquilinum)
Little Gray Polypody (Polypodium polypodioides)
Balsam Fir (Abies balsamea)
Hemlock (Tsuga canadensis)
Red Spruce (Picea rubens)
Ped Pine (Pinus resinosa)
Scrub Pine (Pinus virginiana)
Table Mountain Pine (Pinus pungens)
Lovegrass (Eragrostis hirsuta)
Allegheny fly-back Grass (Danthonia compressa)
Creeping Bent Grass (Agrostis alba var. palustris)
Jack-in-the-Pulpit (Arisaema triphyllum)
Oceanorus (Zygadenus leimanthoides)
Wood Lily (Lilium philadelphicum)
Fawn Lily (Erythronium americanum)
Yellow Clintonia (Clintonia borealis)
White Clintonia (Clintonia umbellulata)
Snow Trillium (Trillium nivale)

Painted Trillium (Trillium undulatum)
Pink Lady's Slipper (Cypripedium acaule)
Showy Orchis (Orchis spectabilis)
Crested Coralroot (Hexalectris spicata)
Butternut (Juglans cinerea)
Black Birch (Betula lenta)
Yellow Birch (Betula lutea)
Paper Birch (Betula papyrifera)
Speckled Alder (Alnus rugosa)
Beech (Fagus grandifolia)
Chestnut (Castanea dentata)
White Oak (Quercus alba)
Chestnut Oak (Quercus montana)
Red Oak (Quercus rubra)
Black Oak (Quercus velutina)
Scrub Oak (Quercus ilicifolia)
Dwarf Hackberry (Celtis occidentalis)
Dutchman's Pipe (Aristolochia durior)
Yellow Buckwheat (Eriogonum alleni)
Slender Knotweed (Polygonum tenue)
Spring Beauty (Claytonia virginica)
Silvery Whitlow-wort (Paronychia argyrocoma)
Mountain Whitlow-wort (Paronychia montana)
Wild Pink (Silene caroliniana)
Roundlobe Hepatica (Hepatica americana)
Sharplobe Hepatica (Hepatica acutiloba)
White-haired Clematis (Clematis albicoma)
Columbine (Aquilegia canadensis)
White Monkshood (Aconitum reclinatum)
Black Cohosh (Cimicifuga racemosa)
Twinleaf (Jeffersonia diphylla)
Blue Cohosh (Caulophyllum thalictroides)
Mountain Magnolia (Magnolia fraseri)
Yellow Poplar (Liriodendron tulipifera)
Pawpaw (Asimina triloba)
Bloodroot (Sanguinaria canadensis)
Wild Bleeding Heart (Dicentra eximia)
Skunk Currant (Ribes glandulosum)
Mountain Ash (Pyrus americana)
Red Raspberry (Rubus idaeus var. strigosus)
Black Cherry (Prunus serotina)
Redbud (Cercis canadensis)
Kate's Mountain Clover (Trifolium virginicum)
Aromatic Sumac (Rhus aromatica)

Poison Ivy (Rhus radicans)
Mountain Holly (Ilex montana)
Black Alder (Ilex verticillata)
Wild Holly (Nemopanthus mucronata)
Sugar Maple (Acer saccharum)
Red Maple (Acer rubrum)
Jewelweed (Impatiens capensis)
St. John's-wort (Hypericum sp.)
Bird's-foot Violet (Viola pedata)
Prickly Pear (Opuntia humifusa)
Fireweed (Epilobium angustifolium)
Shale Evening Primrose (Oenothera argillicola)
Ginseng (Panax quinquefolius)
Mountain Pimpernel (Pseudotaenida montana)
Dwarf Cornel (Cornus canadensis)
Flowering Dogwood (Cornus florida)
Rhododendron (Rhododendron maximum)
Flame Azalea (Rhododendron calendulaceum)
Rose Azalea (Rhododendron roseum)
Mountain Laurel (Kalmia latifolia)
Trailing Arbutus (Epigaea repens)
Huckleberry (Gaylussacia sp.)
Blueberry (Vaccinium sp.)
White Ash (Fraxinus americana)
Velvet Bindweed (Convolvulus purshianus)
Scarlet Wild Bergamot (Monarda didyma)
Cardinal Flower (Lobelia cardinalis)
Great Blue Lobelia (Lobelia siphilitica)
Shale Goldenrod (Solidago harrisii)
Shale Ragwort (Senecio antennariifolius)

The nomenclature for birds follows the order of the 5th Edition of the A.O.U. Check-List of North American Birds (1957).

Common Loon (Gavia immer)
Pied-billed Grebe (Podilymbus podiceps)
Green Heron (Butorides virescens)
Black-crowned Night Heron (Nycticorax nycticorax)
Blue-winged Teal (Anas discors)
Wood Duck (Aix sponsa)
Lesser Scaup (Aythya affinis)
Bufflehead (Bucephala albeola)
Ruddy Duck (Oxyura jamaicensis)
Hooded Merganser (Lophodytes cucullatus)

Red-breasted Merganser (Mergus serrator)
Turkey Vulture (Cathartes aura)
Black Vulture (Coragyps atratus)
Red-tailed Hawk (Buteo jamaicensis)
Red-shouldered Hawk (Buteo lineatus)
Broad-winged Hawk (Buteo platypterus)
Golden Eagle (Aquila chrysaetos)
Marsh Hawk (Circus cyaneus)
Sparrow Hawk (Falco sparverius)
Ruffed Grouse (Bonasa umbellus)
Bobwhite (Colinus virginianus)
Wild Turkey (Meleagris gallopavo)
American Woodcock (Philohela minor)
Common Snipe (Capella gallinago)
Spotted Sandpiper (Actitis macularia)
Solitary Sandpiper (Tringa solitaria)
Herring Gull (Larus argentatus)
Bonaparte's Gull (Larus philadelphia)
Mourning Dove (Zenaidura macroura)
Passenger Pigeon (Ectopistes migratorius)
Screech Owl (Otus asio)
Great Horned Owl (Bubo virginianus)
Barred Owl (Strix varia)
Saw-whet Owl (Aegolius acadicus)
Whip-poor-will (Caprimulgus vociferus)
Ruby-throated Hummingbird (Archilochus colubris)
Belted Kingfisher (Megaceryle alcyon)
Pileated Woodpecker (Dryocopus pileatus)
Red-bellied Woodpecker (Centurus carolinus)
Red-headed Woodpecker (Melanerpes erythrocephalus)
Downy Woodpecker (Dendrocopus pubescens)
Eastern Kingbird (Tyrannus tyrannus)
Great Crested Flycatcher (Myiarchus crinitus)
Eastern Phoebe (Sayornis phoebe)
Rough-winged Swallow (Stelgidopteryx ruficollis)
Barn Swallow (Hirundo rustica)
Cliff Swallow (Petrochelidon pyrrhonota)
Purple Martin (Progne subis)
Blue Jay (Cyanocitta cristata)
Common Raven (Corvus corax)
Black-capped Chickadee (Parus atricapillus)
Tufted Titmouse (Parus bicolor)
White-breasted Nuthatch (Sitta carolinensis)
Red-breasted Nuthatch (Sitta canadensis)

Winter Wren (Troglodytpes troglodypes)
Bewick's Wren (Thryomanes bewickii)
Carolina Wren (Thryothorus ludovicianus)
Mockingbird (Mimus polyglottos)
Catbird (Dumetella carolinensis)
Brown Thrasher (Toxostoma rufum)
Robin (Turdus migratorius)
Wood Thrush (Hylocichla mustelina)
Swainson's Thrush (Hylocichla ustulata)
Veery (Hylocichla fuscescens)
Blue-gray Gnatcatcher (Polioptila caerulea)
Golden-crowned Kinglet (Regulus satrapa)
Loggerhead Shrike (Lanius ludovicianus)
Starling (Sturnus vulgaris)
Yellow-throated Vireo (Vireo flavifrons)
Solitary Vireo (Vireo solitarius)
Red-eyed Vireo (Vireo olivaceus)
Black and White Warbler (Mniotilta varia)
Worm-eating Warbler (Helmintheros vermivorus)
Golden-winged Warbler (Vermivora chrysoptera)
Nashville Warbler (Vermivora ruficapilla)
Parula Warbler (Parula americana)
Yellow Warbler (Dendroica petechia)
Magnolia Warbler (Dendroica magnolia)
Black-throated Blue Warbler (Dendroica caerulescens)
Myrtle Warbler (Dendroica coronata)
Black-throated Green Warbler (Dendroica virens)
Cerulean Warbler (Dendroica cerulea)
Blackburnian Warbler (Dendroica fusca)
Chestnut-sided Warbler (Dendroica pensylvanica)
Prairie Warbler (Dendroica discolor)
Ovenbird (Seiurus aurocapillus)
Northern Waterthrush (Seiurus noveboracensis)
Yellowthroat (Geothlypis trichas)
Yellow-breasted Chat (Icteria virens)
Hooded Warbler (Wilsonia citrina)
Canada Warbler (Wilsonia canadensis)
American Redstart (Setophaga ruticilla)
Eastern Meadowlark (Sturnella magna)
Red-winged Blackbird (Agelaius phoeniceus)
Orchard Oriole (Icterus spurius)
Baltimore Oriole (Icterus galbula)
Common Grackle (Quiscalus quiscula)
Brown-headed Cowbird (Molothrus ater)

Cardinal (Richmondena cardinalis)
Rose-breasted Grosbeak (Pheucticus ludovicianus)
Evening Grosbeak (Hesperiphona vespertina)
Purple Finch (Carpodacus purpureus)
Pine Siskin (Spinus pinus)
American Goldfinch (Spinus tristis)
Red Crossbill (Loxia curvirostra)
White-winged Crossbill (Loxia leucoptera)
Rufous-sided Towhee (Pipilo erythrophthalmus)
Savannah Sparrow (Passerculus sandwichensis)
Grasshopper Sparrow (Ammadramus savannarum)
Vesper Sparrow (Pooecetes gramineus)
Lark Sparrow (Chondestes grammacus)
Slate-colored Junco (Junco hyemalis)
White-crowned Sparrow (Zonotrichia leucophrys)
White-throated Sparrow (Zonotrichia albicollis)
Swamp Sparrow (Melospiza georgiana)
Song Sparrow (Melospiza melodia)

The Latin designations for mammals have been taken from The Mammal Guide (1954) by Ralph S. Palmer. In the case of subspecific races of mammals that are no longer found within the state, the nomenclature has been drawn from "An Annotated List of West Virginia Mammals" by Remington Kellogg (1937).

Opossum (Didelphis marsupialis)
Star-nosed Mole (Condylura cristata)
Smoky Shrew (Sorex fumeus)
Little Brown Bat (Myotis lucifugus)
Big-eared Bat (Corynorhinus rafinesquii)
Black Bear (Ursus americanus)
Raccoon (Procyon lotor)
Fisher (Martes pennanti pennanti)
Common Mink (Mustela vison)
Spotted Skunk (Spilogale putorius)
Striped Skunk (Mephitis mephitis)
Red Fox (Vulpes fulva)
Gray Wolf (Canis lupus lycaon)
Mountain Lion (Felis concolor couguar)
Bobcat (Lynx rufus)
Fox Squirrel (Sciurus niger)
Red Squirrel (Tamiasciurus hudsonicus)
Beaver (Castor canadensis)
White-footed Mouse (Peromyscus maniculatus)

Red-backed Mouse (<u>Clethrionomys</u> <u>gapperi</u>)
Porcupine (<u>Erethizon</u> <u>dorsatum</u> <u>dorsatum</u>)
Eastern Cottontail (<u>Sylvilagus</u> <u>floridanus</u>)
Snowshoe Hare (<u>Lepus</u> <u>americanus</u>)
Eastern Elk (<u>Cervus</u> <u>canadensis</u> <u>canadensis</u>)
White-tailed Deer (<u>Odocoileus</u> <u>virginianus</u>)
Woodland Bison (<u>Bison</u> <u>bison</u> <u>pennsylvanicus</u>)

INDEX